THE DAY
THE WORLD
TOOK OFF

THE DAY
THE WORLD
TOOK OFF

The Roots of the Industrial Revolution

Sally and David Dugan

Dedicated to
Dr Kenneth Playfair Duncan, 1924–1999.

FRONTISPIECE: The technological gulf between East and West is illustrated by *Fireworks over Ryogoku Bridge* by Utagawa Hiroshige (1858). Gunpowder is one of the many inventions that originated in the East. The mystery is why the East did not industrialize before the West.

First published in 2000 by Channel 4 Books, an imprint of
  Macmillan Publishers Ltd, 25 Eccleston Place,
  London SW1W 9NF, Basingstoke and Oxford.
www.macmillan.co.uk
Associated companies throughout the world.
ISBN 0 7522 1870 0
Text © Sally and David Dugan, 2000
The right of Sally and David Dugan to be identified as the
  authors of this work has been asserted by them in accordance
  with the Copyright, Designs and Patents Act 1988.

9 8 7 6 5 4 3 2
A CIP catalogue record for this book is available from the
  British Library.
Design by Isobel Gillan
Colour reproduction by Speedscan
Printed in Italy by New Interlitho
Picture credits can be found on page 192

This book accompanies the television series *The Day the World Took Off* made by *Windfall Films* for Channel 4.
Series Producer: David Dugan

CONTENTS

INTRODUCTION

'Begin at the beginning,' the King said, gravely, 'and go on till you come to the end: then stop.'

LEWIS CARROLL: ALICE'S ADVENTURES IN WONDERLAND (1865)

To those brought up on *1066 and All That*, history can seem like an apparently random but orderly procession of Good and Bad Things. Sales of charts of kings and queens, and school rulers bearing dates, suggest that many people still cling to the idea of chronological pegs on which to hang their history.

The revolutionary idea of *The Day the World Took Off* is to stand history on its head. Or, perhaps more accurately, to make it turn cartwheels. From the opening sequences set on *The Day the World Took Off* in 1830, we are offered a fast rewind through some of the defining moments of the Industrial Revolution. First we look back

Reconstruction of the Day the World Took Off.

100 years, then 250, then 500, then 1,000 … until we end up as far back as 8000BC. Then, in the final programme, we track back through those 10,000 years – to the third millennium of the modern era. It is a dizzying perspective, but one that aims to answer the central question: why did a scraggy little rainswept island off the coast of mainland Europe become the first major industrial centre, when so many other parts of the world looked more promising?

Conventional explanations of the causes of the Industrial Revolution look at such issues as population and the availability of natural resources at the crucial time of change in Britain. Some widen the picture to include northern Europe and America. This series takes a more ambitious, global view, bringing together a small group of international academics in an attempt to solve the puzzle of why the Machine Age took place where and when it did. Meeting among the polished wood furniture and heavy oil paintings of King's College, Cambridge, they look for clues to this historical mystery with the meticulous attention to detail of Sherlock Holmes.

The story starts on a single momentous day in Liverpool, a day that shows the best and worst aspects of the Industrial Revolution. The picture then widens out through ever increasing time spans, ending with a breath-takingly global look at the history of the world – from 8000BC to AD2000 and beyond.

One day
100 years
250 years
500 years
1,000 years
10,000 years

7

THE HISTORIANS

Maxine Berg, Professor of History at the University of Warwick, believes that many conventional histories concentrate too much on inventors and their inventions, and not enough on those who created the demand for the goods they produced. They ignore the vital transformation of consumer desires that went with the Industrial Revolution.

Christopher Cullen is a Senior Lecturer in the History of Chinese Science and Medicine at the School of Oriental and African Studies. 'By concentrating solely on the European roots of the Industrial Revolution,' he says, 'we lose sight of the fact that in 1800 the centre of the world economy was still in East Asia – where many technical advances linked to that revolution had already been made.'

Alan Macfarlane, Professor of Anthropological Science at Cambridge, believes the hardest thing is to realize that there is a mystery. 'But if you look at the long history of man, it's just a tiny speck of time since we suddenly seem to have burst the bounds out of an agrarian agricultural world into an industrial, scientific and modern political world.'

Joel Mokyr, Professor of Economics and History at Northwestern University, Illinois, is interested in the political climate that produces inventions. 'As a general rule, the weaker the government, the better it is for innovation. With some notable exceptions, autocratic rulers have tended to be hostile or indifferent to technological change'.

Simon Schaffer, from the History and Philosophy of Science Department at Cambridge, is fascinated by the way our perceptions have changed. 'It is very recent that themes like fate, inevitability, destiny, the blessing of God, providence, have stopped being the privileged ways of explaining what's happened to our nation in the past.'

Chapter One

THE IRON HORSE

ONE DAY

Time: 15 September 1830

Place: Liverpool and Manchester

It was only yesterday; but what a gulf between now and then! Then was the old world. Stage-coaches, more or less swift, riding-horses, pack-horses, highwaymen, knights in armour, Norman invaders, Roman legions, Druids, Ancient Britons painted blue, and so forth – all these belong to the old period. I will concede a halt in the midst of it, and allow that gunpowder and printing tended to modernize the world. But your railroad starts the new era, and we of a certain age belong to the new time and the old one. … We are of the age of steam.

THOMAS CARLYLE: PAST AND PRESENT (1843)

The world's first regular passenger railway cuts a confident swathe through fields outside Liverpool.

The scene is the thriving port of Liverpool, in the early morning of Wednesday, 15 September 1830. Arriving on foot, on horseback, by stage-coach, by sea and by canal, the crowds have been gathering all week for the grand opening of the new Liverpool and Manchester Railway. Lodging houses are full and celebratory banquets are being prepared. The town crier roams the streets, proclaiming the names of the rich and famous.

This was the day that was to be the inauguration of the great age of steam. Even the Duke of Wellington, then the prime minister, was to grace the celebrations with his presence, despite private reservations that the new railways would encourage the lower classes to travel about. The massing crowds expected a spectacular demonstration of the best of British technology, which they undoubtedly received. Yet, as things turned out, the day provided an equally spectacular demonstration of the dark side of the machine.

Among the guests gathering at Liverpool on this day was the fashionable young actress Fanny Kemble. Fresh from her Covent Garden début in the role of Juliet (with her mother as Lady Capulet), this twenty-year-old pin-up girl of the London stage was experiencing her first provincial tour. Theatrical insights aside, industrial England had been a revelation to Fanny. As she wrote rather earnestly to her friend, the phrenologist George Combe: 'These manufacturing towns have afforded me much pleasure and information and as I am rather desirous at present to acquire some knowledge on scientific subjects Liverpool and Manchester and Birmingham have been like the pictures in the children's spelling books, illustrations and encouragement.'

Enthusiastic visions of steam and speed had filled her letters after her first visit to the almost-completed 98 miles of track that made up the Liverpool to Manchester Railway. A keen horsewoman, she described the locomotive that pulled her across the newly laid rails in the only way she knew how:

We were introduced to the little engine which was to drag us along the rails. She (for they make these curious little fire-horses all mares) consisted of a boiler, a stove, a small platform, a bench, and behind the bench a barrel containing enough water to prevent her being thirsty for fifteen miles, – the whole machine not bigger than a common fire-engine. She goes upon two wheels, which are her feet, and are moved by bright steel legs called pistons … the coals, which are its oats, were under the bench, and there was a small glass tube affixed to the boiler, with water in it, which indicates by its fullness or emptiness when the creature wants water, which is immediately conveyed to it from its reservoirs. … This snorting little animal, which I felt rather inclined to pat, was then harnessed to our carriage, and Mr Stephenson having taken me on the bench of the engine with him, we started at about ten miles an hour.
(LETTER TO A FRIEND, 26 AUGUST 1830)

The actress Fanny Kemble — seen here in her role as Juliet — was enraptured after her first ride on a 'fire-horse', and gave lively accounts of the early days of the railway in her letters and journals.

Fanny Kemble fell in love not only with this 'magical machine, with its flying white breath', but with the railway's creator, George Stephenson, and the sheer thrill of travelling at a hitherto undreamed-of speed of 35 miles per hour. Reassuring her friend that the engine really did travel faster than a bird (for they had tried the experiment with a snipe), her letter went on:

You cannot conceive what that sensation of cutting the air was; the motion is as smooth as possible, too. I could either have read or written; and, as it was, I stood up, and with my bonnet off 'drank the air before me'. The wind, which was strong, or perhaps the force of our thrusting against it, absolutely weighted my eyelids down. When I closed my eyes this sensation of flying was quite delightful, and strange beyond description; yet, strange as it was, I had a perfect sense of security, and not the slightest fear.

If the year 1830 had been a momentous one for Fanny Kemble, it was a turning point for others, too. It was a year that saw the death of the old King, George IV, whose bibulous lifestyle is so memorably described by Mrs Harriet Arbuthnot, an acute observer of the court and social scene.

[23 April] He gets black in the face & his pulse alters when he has these attacks on his breath, which they think shows something wrong about the heart. They took him out airing ten days ago &, when he got to the Lodge, he was so bad they were frightful to death & thought he would die. They gave him quantities of brandy, & he rallied so completely that he got into his carriage & drove 20 miles …

One night he drank two glasses of hot ale & toast, three glasses of claret, some strawberries!! and a glass of brandy. Last night they gave him some physic and, after it, he drank three glasses of port wine & a glass of brandy. No wonder he is likely to die! But they say he will have these things & nobody can prevent him. I dare say the wine would not hurt him, for with the Evil (which all the Royal Family have) it is necessary, I believe, to have a great deal of high food, but the mixture of ale & strawberries is enough to kill a horse …
[16 July] I went yesterday to Windsor to the funeral of the late King. … The coffin was very fine and a most enormous size. They were very near having a frightful accident for, when the body was in the leaden coffin, the lead was observed to have bulged very considerably & in fact was in great danger of bursting. They were obliged to puncture the lead to let out the air & then to fresh cover it with lead. Rather an unpleasant operation, *I should think, but the embalming must have been very ill done.*

The year 1830 also saw agricultural riots, and the publication of *Rural Rides* by William Cobbett, a lament for a vanishing way of life, and a call to action. Cobbett was a farmer at heart and a politician by chance, and his account of a fact-finding journey through southern England is punctuated by harangues to unsuspecting rustics and readers alike.

Showing the same disdain for turnpike roads that a modern traveller might show for motorways, Cobbett took a nostalgic journey on horseback through the byways and fields of rural England. Travelling with his son, he pointed out essential landmarks – including the sand-hill which he and his brothers used to slide down.

This was the spot where I was receiving my education; and this was the sort of education; and I am perfectly satisfied that if I had not received such an education, or something very much like it; that, if I had been brought up a milksop, with a nursery-maid everlastingly at my heels; I should have been at this day as great a fool, as inefficient a mortal, as any of those frivolous idiots that are turned out from Winchester and Westminster School, or from any of those dens of dunces called colleges and Universities. It is impossible to say how much I owe to that sand-hill; and I went to return it my thanks for the ability which it probably gave me to be one of the greatest terrors, to one of the greatest and most powerful bodies of knaves and fools, that ever were permitted to afflict this or any other country.

Cobbett blamed industrialization – which he castigated as 'The Thing' – for Britain's misfortunes. Certainly, his comments on some of the more ludicrous aspect of rural economics may strike sympathetic chords with farmers today. At Arundel, he wrote:

As I was coming into this town I saw a new-fashioned sort of stone-cracking. *A man had a* sledge-hammer, *and was cracking the* heads *of the big stones that had been* laid on the road a good while ago. *This is a very good way; but, this man told me, that he was set at this, because the* farmers *had no employment for many of the men.* 'Well,' said I, 'but they pay you to do this!' 'Yes,' *he said.* 'Well, then,' said I, 'is it not better for them to pay you for *working on their land?'* 'I can't tell, indeed, Sir, how that is.' *But, only think; there is* half the hay-making to do: *I saw, while I was talking to this man, fifty people in one hay-field of Lord Egremont, making and carrying hay; and yet, at a season like this, the farmers are so poor as to be unable to pay the labourers to work on the land!*

George Stephenson (1781–1848), the blunt, self-educated railway engineer whose enthusiasm captured Fanny Kemble's imagination.

This year also brought a new edition of an essay on population by the man Cobbett scornfully referred to as Parson Malthus. The Reverend Thomas Malthus – arguably one of the most misrepresented writers in history – painted a grim picture of a poverty- and disease-ridden future if population growth was not curbed. He preached a gospel of moral restraint, encouraging people to limit their families in the face of fears that the numbers of mouths to feed would outstrip food supplies.

The atmosphere that led to his doom-laden prophecies can easily be understood by looking at two of the fastest-growing areas of Britain in 1830: the cities of Liverpool and Manchester. For in both places, there was a huge gulf between the grandeur of the public buildings and the dark hopelessness of the back streets.

Liverpool was already a well-established port, described by Lord Erskine in 1792 as an 'immense place standing like another Venice on the waters … glittering with the cheerful habitations of well-protected men – the busy seat of trade, and the gay seat of elegant amusements growing out of its prosperity – illuminated by the cheerful face of industry'.

Historically, slavery had played an important role in the triangular commerce that created Liverpool's wealth. During the eighteenth century, ships had carried cotton goods and hardware from Liverpool to West Africa, slaves from West Africa to the West Indies and Virginia, then sugar, rum, tobacco and raw cotton back to Liverpool. After the abolition of the slave trade, however, commentators preferred to dwell on the results of the port's wealth, rather than its causes. The author of *Gore's Liverpool Directory for 1832*, for example, simply notes: 'This trade [slavery] was found to be most lucrative, and to wonderfully advance the wealth and revenue of the Port, over it however, the philanthropist gladly flings the mantle of oblivion, and hails with rapture that act of a British Senate which puts its Ban upon the traffic in "human sinews and human blood".'

After a catalogue of facts and figures about the depth of the estuary and the frequency of tides, he goes on to give an exhaustive inventory of everything from the Liverpool Baths, with their rusticated walls, piazzas and colonnades, to the tobacco warehouses. The tone throughout is one of fulsome praise.

The stranger on entering Liverpool finds much to arrest his attention. … Does he land upon its quays, he is animated by a view of a 'forest fleet', which exhibits the extent of those numerous docks that seem destined for an enlarged and wide spreading commerce. The busy hum of traffic is heard on every side, and the genius of industry seems to smile upon the efforts of her votaries. Ascending further into the town, he is struck by the magnificent structures and noble streets that meet his eye, while the air of fashion, splendour of equipage and brilliancy of the tout ensemble, *recall many capitals to his recollection, and show that from pride of imitation the inhabitants have been most successful in their ambitions of equality. The streets are wide, and admirably calculated for health and comfort … [The houses] for the gentry, and principal merchants, are upon an enlarged scale, comprise several suites of rooms, and are fitted up in a style corresponding to the wealth and dignity of the owners. The others vary in their degrees of magnitude, according to the rank of the occupants, but all shew in their different arrangements that due regard has been paid to what an Englishman knows so well how to prize the comforts of his own fireside. ...*

The places of Public Amusement in Liverpool are numerous, the Reading-rooms extensive, the Scientific Institutions many, and the taste for literature progressing with considerable activity.

With its dramatic site, rising on a series of steps above the broad Mersey estuary, Liverpool in 1830 was a thriving port. A total of 11,214 ships passed through the imposing gates and swivel bridges of its nine working docks during the year. (The ninth dock, Clarence Dock, was opened just the day after the new Liverpool and Manchester Railway, to accommodate the growing traffic from Ireland.) The sheer scale of the city's public face, with its imposing classically influenced buildings, inspired confidence.

However, the city's rapid growth had a price. In 1700, Liverpool had a population of 5,145. By 1821 it had reached 118,972, increasing by 40 per cent over the succeeding decade, with inevitable human consequences. About one in nine people were living in cellars. In poorer areas the water supply was owned by two companies, which turned on the water only twice a week, for half an hour at a time.

This painting of the Liverpool docks by John Atkinson Grimshaw shows the bustling, gas-lit streets and classical buildings that went with proud prosperity. However, home for many workers was a dingy cellar with no running water.

Manchester – Liverpool's upstart rival – had become the greatest centre of population outside London by 1830, and had suffered even more from the inevitable squalor that came with random, unplanned growth. This made it the natural focus for the young radical German writer, Friedrich Engels, in *The Condition of the Working Class in England*, written when he was just twenty-four, and published in 1845. After a catalogue of depressing detail about back-street pigsties and offal heaps, he writes:

Such is the Old Town of Manchester, and on re-reading my description, I am forced to admit that instead of being exaggerated, it is far from black enough to convey a true impression of the filth, ruin, and uninhabitableness, the defiance of all considerations of cleanliness, ventilation, and health which characterize the construction of this single district, containing at least twenty to thirty thousand inhabitants. And such a district exists in the heart of the second city of England, the first manufacturing city of the world. If anyone wishes to see in how little space a human being can move, how little air – and such air! – he can breathe, how little of civilization he may share and yet live, it is only necessary to travel hither. True, this is the Old *Town, and the people of Manchester emphasize the fact whenever anyone mentions to them the frightful condition of this hell upon earth; but what does that prove? Everything which here arouses horror and indignation is of recent origin, belongs to the* industrial epoch.

Dr James Kay – later Sir James Kay-Shuttleworth – provided graphic descriptions of living conditions in the dingy workers' tenements that sprang up around the factories: 'The houses are ill-soughed, often ill ventilated, unprovided with privies, and in consequence the streets, which are narrow, unpaved and worn into deep ruts, become the common receptacles of mud, refuse and disgusting ordure.'

Dr Kay experienced the consequences of such insanitary conditions first hand when he was called upon to attend Manchester's first victim of cholera, a highly infectious disease spread by eating food or drinking water contaminated with faeces. In a manuscript written many years later, he described the inevitability of its progress:

On my arrival in a two-roomed house, I found an Irishman lying on a bed close to the window. The temperature of his skin was somewhat lower than usual, the pulse was weak and quick. He complained of no pain. The face was rather pale, and the man much dejected. None of the characteristic symptoms of cholera had occurred, but his attendant told me that the strength had gradually declined during the day, and that, seeing no cause for it, he had formed a suspicion of contagion. I sat by the man's bed for an hour, during which the pulse became gradually weaker. In a second hour it was almost extinct, and it became apparent that the patient would die. His wife and three

The smoking chimneys of Manchester, nicknamed Cottonopolis after its major industry. At the heart of the canal system in the eighteenth century, its rapid growth continued after the opening of the Liverpool to Manchester Railway. Overcrowded and insanitary, the city's name became synonymous in many people's minds with dirt and disease. John Ruskin talked of 'Manchester devil's darkness'.

children were in the room, and she was prepared by us for the too probable event. Thus the afternoon slowly passed away, and as evening approached I sent the young surgeon to have in readiness the cholera van not far away. We were surrounded by an excitable Irish population, and it was obviously desirable to remove the body as soon as possible, and then the family, and to lock up the house before any alarm was given. As twilight came on the sufferer expired without cramp or any other characteristic symptom. The wife had been soothed and she readily consented to be removed with her children to the hospital. Then suddenly the van drew up at the door, and in one minute, before the Irish were aware, drove away with its sad burden.

No case of Asiatic cholera had occurred in Manchester, yet notwithstanding the total absence of characteristic symptoms in this case, I was convinced that the contagion had arrived, and the patient had been its victim. The Knott Hill Hospital was a cotton factory stripped of its machinery, and furnished with iron bedsteads and bedding on every floor. On my arrival here I found the widow and her three children with a nurse grouped round a fire at one end of a gloomy ward. I ascertained that all necessary arrangements had been made for their comfort. They had an evening meal; the children were put to bed near the fire, except the infant which I left lying upon its mother's lap. None of them showed any signs of disease, and I left the ward to take some refreshment. On my return, or at a later visit before midnight, the infant had been sick in its mother's lap, had made a faint cry and had died. The mother was naturally full of terror and distress, for the child had had no medicine, had been fed only from its mother's breast, and, consequently, she could have no doubt that it perished from the same causes as its father. I sat with her and the nurse by the fire very late into the night. While I was there the children did not wake, nor seem in any way disturbed, and at length I thought I might myself seek some repose. When I returned about six o'clock in the morning, another child had severe cramps with some sickness, and while I stood by the bedside, it died. Then, later, the third and eldest child had all the characteristic symptoms of cholera and perished in one or two hours. In the course of the day the mother likewise suffered from a severe and rapid succession of the characteristic symptoms and died, so that within twenty-four hours the whole family was extinct, and it was not known that any other case of cholera had occurred in Manchester or its vicinity. …

The cholera epidemic of 1832 was the first of four major outbreaks in the nineteenth century that killed over 30,000 people nationwide. Not even the most revisionist historian would contest the fact that diseases like cholera and typhus were major killers in poor areas. However, epidemics that could wipe out whole populations were rare. It seems that, unlike towns in other countries, British cities could grow into big sewers and still remain relatively healthy places to live in.

Alan Macfarlane, one of our historians, thinks he knows why British cities did not turn into diseased cesspools during the Industrial Revolution. His answer comes from a surprising source: our drinking habits. It seems that the British fondness for beer and tea could have been a life-saver. Water is a major source of infection, but the process of making both drinks involves boiling water, thus killing harmful germs. In his book, *The Savage Wars of Peace*, Professor Macfarlane cites the surprise of the French traveller, César de Saussure, who wrote in 1726:

Would you believe it, though water is to be had in abundance in London, and of fairly good quality, absolutely none is drunk? The lower classes, even the paupers, do not know what it is to quench their thirst with water. In this country nothing but beer is drunk, and it is made in several qualities. Small beer is what everyone drinks when thirsty; it is used even in the best houses, and costs only a penny the pot. Another kind of beer is called porter, meaning carrier, because the greater quantity of this beer is consumed by the working classes.

Even charity children were given small beer rather than water, until around the middle of the eighteenth century, when tea took over as the national drink of preference. Samuel Johnson admitted that he was 'a hardened and shameless Tea-drinker, who has for twenty years diluted his meals with only the infusion of this fascinating plant, whose kettle has scarcely had time to cool, who with Tea amuses the evening, with Tea solaces the midnight, and with Tea welcomes the morning'.

To those who would argue that tea was too expensive to be drunk in large quantities, Alan Macfarlane points to evidence that suggests that poorer people drank an extremely weak brew, just coloured with a few leaves of the cheapest tea. Like beer, tea had the advantage of being made from boiled water – and containing tannin, a phenolic substance that can act like a mild antiseptic and prevent the spreading of germs inside the body.

Professor Macfarlane has made a detailed comparative study of Britain and Japan, and it was this that led him to develop his theory about the way our drinking habits have kept us healthy. Both countries have historically had relatively low rates of mortality – and tea drinking was one very obvious thing they had in common. As he put it: 'When the Japanese population were drinking tea, they were also daily drinking pints of powerful antiseptic.'

So Japan, like Britain, was relatively free from disease. It had a healthy, willing, working population. In 1830, Tokyo was a busy trade centre, and as big a city as London. Yet Japan had to wait almost half a century for its Industrial Revolution. While Britain had its *Rocket*, Japan not only had no railways or engines, its people didn't even see the need for wheels! We will explore the roots of this difference – which take us back through a thousand years of Japanese history – in Chapters Four and Five.

In *1066 and All That*, W. C. Sellar and R. J. Yeatman have their own name for the Industrial Revolution in Britain: the 'Industrial Revelation'. It was a time, as they describe it, when 'many very remarkable discoveries and inventions were made. Most memorable among these was the discovery (made by all the rich men in England at once) that women and children could work for twenty-five hours a day in factories without many of them dying or becoming excessively deformed. This was known as the Industrial Revelation and completely changed the faces of the North of England.'

The historian E. J. Hobsbawm coined the phrase that has become almost a cliché of history: 'Whoever says Industrial Revolution says cotton'. And many of the most dramatic accounts of the advent of the machine in the 1830s came from the new heartland of cotton manufacture: Manchester. In *The Moral and Physical Conditions of the Working Classes employed in the Cotton Manufacture in Manchester*, published in 1832 (the same year as the cholera epidemic), Sir James Kay-Shuttleworth wrote: 'Whilst the engine runs the people must work – men, women, and children are yoked together with iron and steam. The animal machine – breakable in the best case, subject to a thousand sources of suffering – is chained fast to the iron machine, which knows no suffering and no weariness. …'

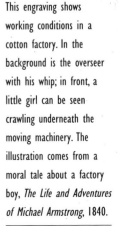

This engraving shows working conditions in a cotton factory. In the background is the overseer with his whip; in front, a little girl can be seen crawling underneath the moving machinery. The illustration comes from a moral tale about a factory boy, *The Life and Adventures of Michael Armstrong*, 1840.

Other contemporary accounts strike a note of awe – but, intentionally or unintentionally, also convey a sense of the inhuman face of mechanization. Edward Baines of the *Leeds Mercury*, in his *History of the Cotton Manufacture in Great Britain*, wrote in 1835:

It is by iron fingers, teeth, and wheels, moving with exhaustless energy and devouring speed, that the cotton is opened, cleaned, spread, carded, drawn, roved, spun, wound, warped, dressed, and woven. … All are moving at once – the operations chasing each other; and all derive their motion from the mighty engine, which, firmly seated in the lower part of the building, and constantly fed with water and fuel, toils through the day with the strength of perhaps a hundred horses. Men, in the meanwhile, have merely to attend on this wonderful series of mechanisms, to supply it with work, and to check its slight and infrequent regularities – each workman performing, or rather superintending, as much work as could have been done by two or three hundred men *sixty years ago.*

Modern historians tend to play down the impact of the factory by 1830, emphasizing that hand labour and outwork in country areas still had an important part to play. But there is no doubt that the lives of the thousands who were drawn to the new industrial areas were changed for ever. Fed by water, steam and labour, the mills were demanding taskmasters. Whole families spent almost all of their waking hours tending to the new generation of textile machinery, and children as young as six were given menial tasks like scavenging cotton fluff from beneath the moving machinery. It was dirty work.

By the end of a working day, workers in a cotton mill looked like snowmen from the cotton fibres in the air. Carding room operatives suffered from breathlessness due to a disease that later became known as card-room asthma, and tended to die young. Noise levels were such that a system of sign language was invented, and hearing loss was common. Machine operatives were not allowed to leave their post even to go the toilet without permission from the overseer. A woman would carry on working until the full nine months of pregnancy, and would return to work the week after giving birth for fear of losing her job. She would hope for an indulgent overseer who would let her nurse the new baby.

A particular problem in cotton mills was maintaining the humidity that was needed to prevent the cotton threads from breaking. Weavers would stand on planks raised up from floor level, and the room would be heated by a network of pipes, creating steam. Buckets of water would be thrown on to the floor to keep up the sauna atmosphere. In the summer, temperatures could reach more than 26 degrees centigrade, or, 80 degrees Fahrenheit. In the winter, the opposite was the case, as one woman from Colne recalled: 'There was just enough heat to keep the yarn happy. In the cold, the ends kept dropping down. I used to dread it. Everything was cold, and your hands were soon cold because everything about a Lancashire loom was made of iron. You could hardly tie knots because your hands were frozen.'

Working for twelve hours under these conditions was not only unpleasant, but dangerous, as Friedrich Engels saw at first hand when his research for *The Condition of the Working Class in England* led him to take a job in a Manchester cotton mill.

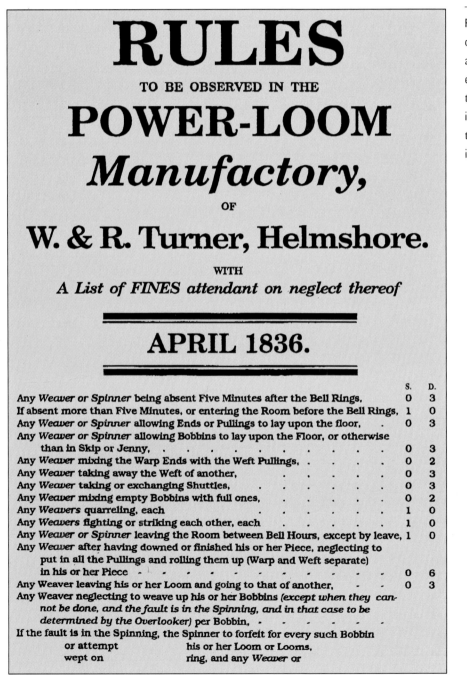

Rules, strictly enforced by overseers, aimed to produce a generation of workers as efficient as the machines they tended. There is information missing at the bottom, as the poster is torn.

RULES

TO BE OBSERVED IN THE

POWER-LOOM

Manufactory,

OF

W. & R. Turner, Helmshore.

WITH

A List of FINES attendant on neglect thereof

APRIL 1836.

	S.	D.
Any *Weaver* or *Spinner* being absent Five Minutes after the Bell Rings,	0	3
If absent more than Five Minutes, or entering the Room before the Bell Rings,	1	0
Any *Weaver* or *Spinner* allowing Ends or Pullings to lay upon the floor,	0	3
Any *Weaver* or *Spinner* allowing Bobbins to lay upon the Floor, or otherwise than in Skip or Jenny,	0	3
Any *Weaver* mixing the Warp Ends with the Weft Pullings,	0	2
Any *Weaver* taking away the Weft of another,	0	3
Any *Weaver* taking or exchanging Shuttles,	0	3
Any *Weaver* mixing empty Bobbins with full ones,	0	2
Any *Weavers* quarreling, each	1	0
Any *Weavers* fighting or striking each other, each	1	0
Any *Weaver* or *Spinner* leaving the Room between Bell Hours, except by leave,	1	0
Any *Weaver* after having downed or finished his or her Piece, neglecting to put in all the Pullings and rolling them up (Warp and Weft separate) in his or her Piece	0	6
Any Weaver leaving his or her Loom and going to that of another,	0	3

Any Weaver neglecting to weave up his or her Bobbins *(except when they cannot be done, and the fault is in the Spinning, and in that case to be determined by the Overlooker)* per Bobbin,

If the fault is in the Spinning, the Spinner to forfeit for every such Bobbin
     or attempt   his or her Loom or Looms,
     wept on   ring, and any *Weaver* or

In the throstle-room of the cotton mill at Manchester, in which I was employed, I do not remember to have seen one single tall, well-built girl; they were all short, dumpy, and badly-formed, decidedly ugly in the whole development of the figure. But apart from all these diseases and malformations, the limbs of the operatives suffer in still another way. Work among the machines gives rise to multitudes of accidents of more or less serious nature, which have for the operative the secondary effect of unfitting him for his work more or less completely. The most common accident is the crushing of a single joint of a finger, somewhat less common the loss of the whole finger, half or a whole hand, an arm, etc., in the machinery. Lock-jaw very often follows, even upon the lesser among these injuries, and brings death with it. Besides the deformed persons, a great number of maimed ones may be seen going about in Manchester; this one has lost an arm or a part of one, that one a foot, the third half a leg; it is like living in the midst of an army just returned from a campaign.

However, not all factory owners were the heartless capitalists that Engels implied. While moves among philanthropists led to a series of Factory Reform Acts, designed to limit the working day and ensure the education of factory children, some employers were taking matters into their own hands. One of the best-known examples is at Quarry Bank Mill in Styal, Cheshire, one of Britain's largest historic working cotton mills, now owned by the National Trust. Visitors can still see the Apprentice House which was home to a hundred pauper children, who worked for up to thirteen hours in the mill by day and had a ragged schooling by night. They slept two to a bed and had clean sheets once a month but, by the standards of the time, the mill owner was not a hard taskmaster. The mill and its surrounding model village, in its green riverside setting, was in fact something of a showpiece.

Andrew Ure, a professor at the University of Glasgow, was an enthusiastic supporter of ventures such as that at Styal. In *The Philosophy of Manufactures*, published in 1835, he quoted with approval the Sunday churchgoing behaviour of the young factory apprentices: 'The Sunday scholars, equally numerous, belonging to the rural population, appeared to great disadvantage alongside of the factory children, the former being worse clad and worse looking than the latter, and worse behaved during divine service.'

He went on to describe in some detail the educational and domestic arrangements for the apprentices (including the fact that they had bacon every day).

The Messrs. Greg [factory owners] are in the habit of looking after the education of the boys, and their sisters superintend that of the girls, who are taught reading, writing, arithmetic, sewing, and other domestic avocations. The health of these apprentices is unequalled by that of any other class of work-people in any occupation. The medical certificate laid before the Factory Commissioners proves that the deaths are only one in 150, being no more than one-third of the average of Lancashire.

Such mill owners thought they offered a fair bargain: houses, gardens and schools in return for hard and dangerous work. In any event, workers increasingly had little choice. Before factories, the textile industry had relied on skilled outworkers. But since an unskilled power-loom operator in a factory could produce ten times more cloth than a weaver at home, the factories increasingly won the day. Wages hit rock bottom, falling by 60 per cent in twenty years. A series of trade depressions did not help and, since the home cotton weavers were concentrated within a relatively limited area, whole communities could easily be thrown into the gloom of unemployment. On the first Sunday of May 1829, for example, no banns of marriage were called at Burnley parish church, although the average each Sunday was normally between fifteen and twenty couples. A report in the *Blackburn Mail* of 6 May 1829 commented: 'No other reason can be given for this unusual circumstance, except that the extreme poverty and wretchedness of the working people now prevent them marrying.'

Worries about the break-up of the family, and the desertion of the closely knit village communities for the impersonality of the big towns were widespread. Families no longer measured out their days by the march of the sun across the sky, or their months by the rhythm of the seasons. Factory

Modern reconstruction of working conditions at Quarry Bank Mill in Cheshire.

The railway engine as fairground novelty: Richard Trevithick's *Catch-Me-If-You-Can* at Euston Square, London, in 1809. Trevithick (1771–1833) was a Cornishman who devoted his life to the improvement of the steam engine, but recognition eluded him.

hooters and bells dominated everything, as factory owners wanted to make sure they got value for money from workers and machines alike. If you were five minutes late for work, you were fined; oddly enough, if you were at your post too early, you were also fined. In a very real sense, time was money.

Measuring time accurately became more important than ever before. The old system of local time, where virtually every other civic clock was set to a different time, became increasingly incompatible with efficiency. In the absence of a national time zone, stage-coach drivers used to have special watches that were set to run fast or slow depending on the direction in which they were travelling. This was just about workable in 1750, when the journey from London to Manchester took eighty hours. But by 1845 the new, efficient railway network could cover the same distance in just eight hours. A better time-keeping system was essential, hence the introduction of Railway Time.

In the West, the growing obsession with time generated a whole new way of life that encompassed the Protestant work ethic and provides one obvious solution to the riddle of what caused the Industrial Revolution. Another solution is provided by the technology of time. In the China of 1830, clocks were simply toys that were kept in a box in the Emperor's palace. (We'll see in Chapter Four how this partly explains five centuries of Chinese technological stagnation.)

Strange as it may now seem, in the nineteenth century Britain led the world in clock-making, and Liverpool was a major centre for this. By the year 1800, nearly 2,000 hands were employed in the trade. Liverpool clock-makers produced on average 150 watches a week, and built up such a high reputation that they even managed to export their movements to Geneva.

Simon Schaffer has a theory that part of the solution to the Industrial Revolution riddle lies in British technical expertise in three apparently unrelated areas: cannons, clocks and beer. To take the example of steam locomotives like the *Rocket*: British cannon-makers had pioneered the kind of precision engineering needed to make pistons that fit exactly inside their cylinders to form an airtight seal. British clock-makers knew how to translate up and down movement of big levers into a circular motion. And British brewers had worked out how to keep steam pressure constant, so it did not blow up in your face. Once more, the story seems to come back to beer!

Steam has a vital place in most people's mental image of the Industrial Revolution, and the *Rocket* is a key icon. But it was only by a combination of historical chance and canny showmanship by George Stephenson, the man known as the father of our railways, that it gained its unique position.

The idea of the steam locomotive was not new. Richard Trevithick, a Cornish mine engineer, had designed a locomotive to pull a 10-ton load on a 10-mile track between Penydarren ironworks at Merthyr Tydfil and the Glamorganshire canal in 1804. Sceptics, not understanding the laws of friction, had been unable to see how smooth iron wheels could run on smooth rails without slipping, but he proved them wrong. However, his invention does not seem to have been taken that seriously – not helped, perhaps, by a misguided attempt at publicity, when he brought a locomotive to London and offered rides as a tourist attraction.

George Stephenson, by contrast, had an eye for the right kind of publicity, and an ambitious vision that made him the Richard Branson of his day. That potent Victorian myth-maker, Samuel Smiles, seized so successfully on the story of this collier's son made good that it is only recently that historians have started to realize the extent to which his reputation has eclipsed that of his son, Robert Stephenson, and his other collaborators. 'RAIL HISTORIANS GIVE STEPHENSON THE ROCKET', ran the headline on an article in the *Independent* on 11 September 1998, which claimed that Stephenson should share the honours on the £5 note with other engineers. One Durham-based historian compared Stephenson to today's Japanese car

Robert Stephenson (1803–1859), designer of the *Rocket*, whose reputation was somewhat eclipsed by that of his father George. In later life he went on to become a bridge builder and politician.

manufacturers: 'He went around looking at other people's inventions and said, "That looks good, I'll use that bit and that bit."'

As chief engineer to the Stockton and Darlington Railway, opened in 1825, and the Liverpool and Manchester Railway, George Stephenson undoubtedly oversaw some spectacular feats of engineering. But his son, Robert, should take the credit for the *Rocket*, whose victory at the celebrated Rainhill trials ensured a future for steam locomotives.

The Liverpool and Manchester Railway was all but built when its directors turned their attention to what kind of power should be used on its rails. They offered a prize of £500 for a 'Locomotive Engine which shall be a decided improvement on those now in use ...'. The advertisement, addressed to Engineers and Iron Founders, appeared in the *Liverpool Mercury* on 1 May 1829. Rival engines were to compete over a length of level track on the Manchester side of Rainhill bridge. Each engine was not to exceed 6 tons in weight, have a working steam pressure of no more than 50 pounds per square inch, and was not to cost more than £550 to build. The test was ten double runs with a set load at full speed over one and a half miles of track. After a pause to take on fuel and water, the trial was to be repeated, the distance being the equivalent to the return journey between Manchester and Liverpool.

The competition produced a bizarre variety of entries, as Henry Booth, the railway treasurer, recalled:

From professors of philosophy, down to the humblest mechanic all were zealous in their proffers of assistance. England, America and Continental Europe were alike tributary. Every element and almost every substance were brought into requisition and made subservient to the great work. The friction of carriages was to be reduced so low that a silk thread would draw them, and the power to be applied was to be so vast as to rend a cable asunder. Hydrogen gas and high-pressure steam – columns of water and columns of mercury – a hundred atmospheres and a perfect vacuum – machines working in a circle without fire or steam, generating power at one end of the process and giving it out at the other – wheels within wheels, to multiply speed without diminishing power – with every complication of balancing and counteravailing forces, to be the ne plus ultra *of perpetual motion.*

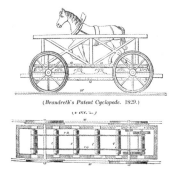

(Brandreth's Patent Cyclopede. 1829.)

ABOVE: The horse-powered *Cyclopede*, invented by a Liverpool barrister, proved impractical when the horse fell through the drive belt after reaching a speed of only five miles per hour.

It is interesting that many contemporary accounts of the nine-day trials – which attracted crowds variously estimated as being from ten to fifteen thousand people – make it sound like a horse race. Indeed the *Cyclopede* – entered by T. S. Brandreth, one of the Liverpool and Manchester directors – *was* little more than a light cart powered by a treadmill worked by two horses. There was also a *Manumotive Carriage*, propelled by two men. However, doubts about the practicality of the *Cyclopede*, and the morality of using men like animals in the *Manumotive*, eliminated these at an early stage.

1829.

GRAND COMPETITION

OF

LOCOMOTIVES

ON THE

LIVERPOOL & MANCHESTER RAILWAY.

STIPULATIONS & CONDITIONS

On which the Directors of the Liverpool and Manchester Railway offer a Premium of £500 for the most Improved Locomotive Engine.

I.

The said Engine must "effectually consume its own smoke," according to the provisions of the Railway Act, 7th Geo. IV.

II.

The Engine, if it weighs Six Tons, must be capable of drawing after it, day by day, on a well-constructed Railway, on a level plane, a Train of Carriages of the gross weight of Twenty Tons, including the Tender and Water Tank, at the rate of Ten Miles per Hour, with a pressure of steam in the boiler not exceeding Fifty Pounds on the square inch.

III.

There must be Two Safety Valves, one of which must be completely out of the reach or control of the Engine-man, and neither of which must be fastened down while the Engine is working.

IV.

The Engine and Boiler must be supported on Springs, and rest on Six Wheels; and the height from the ground to the top of the Chimney must not exceed Fifteen Feet.

V.

The weight of the Machine, WITH ITS COMPLEMENT OF WATER in the Boiler, must, at most, not exceed Six Tons, and a Machine of less weight will be preferred if it draw AFTER it a PROPORTIONATE weight; and if the weight of the Engine, &c., do not exceed FIVE TONS, then the gross weight to be drawn need not exceed Fifteen Tons; and in that proportion for Machines of still smaller weight—provided that the Engine, &c., shall still be on six wheels, unless the weight (as above) be reduced to Four Tons and a Half, or under, in which case the Boiler, &c., may be placed on four wheels. And the Company shall be at liberty to put the Boiler, Fire Tube, Cylinders, &c., to the test of a pressure of water not exceeding 150 Pounds per square inch, without being answerable for any damage the Machine may receive in consequence.

VI.

There must be a Mercurial Gauge affixed to the Machine, with Index Rod, showing the Steam Pressure above 45 Pounds per square inch; and constructed to blow out a Pressure of 60 Pounds per inch.

VII.

The Engine to be delivered complete for trial, at the Liverpool end of the Railway, not later than the 1st of October next.

VIII.

The price of the Engine which may be accepted, not to exceed £550, delivered on the Railway; and any Engine not approved to be taken back by the Owner.

N.B.—The Railway Company will provide the ENGINE TENDER with a supply of Water and Fuel, for the experiment. The distance within the Rails is four feet eight inches and a half.

THE LOCOMOTIVE STEAM ENGINES,

WHICH COMPETED FOR THE PRIZE OF £500 OFFERED BY THE DIRECTORS OF THE LIVERPOOL AND MANCHESTER RAILWAY COMPANY.

DRAWN TO A SCALE ¼ INCH TO A FOOT.

THE "ROCKET" OF M.R ROB.T STEPHENSON OF NEWCASTLE,

WHICH DRAWING A LOAD EQUIVALENT TO THREE TIMES ITS WEIGHT TRAVELLED AT THE RATE OF 12½ MILES AN HOUR, AND WITH A CARRIAGE & PASSENGERS AT THE RATE OF 24 MILES. COST PER MILE FOR FUEL ABOUT THREE HALFPENCE.

THE "NOVELTY" OF MESS.RS BRAITHWAITE & ERRICSSON OF LONDON,

WHICH DRAWING A LOAD EQUIVALENT TO THREE TIMES ITS WEIGHT TRAVELLED AT THE RATE OF 20¾ MILES AN HOUR, AND WITH A CARRIAGE & PASSENGERS AT THE RATE OF 32 MILES. COST PER MILE FOR FUEL ABOUT ONE HALFPENNY.

THE "SANSPAREIL" OF M.R HACKWORTH OF DARLINGTON,

WHICH DRAWING A LOAD EQUIVALENT TO THREE TIMES ITS WEIGHT TRAVELLED AT THE RATE OF 12½ MILES AN HOUR. COST FOR FUEL PER MILE ABOUT TWO PENCE.

The more serious contenders were the giant iron horses of the steam age: the *Rocket*; the *Sans Pareil* (which was actually declared overweight, but allowed to run); the *Perseverance* (which was damaged on the way to the trials, and could do no better than 6 miles an hour); and the *Novelty*. The *Novelty* was initially the crowd's favourite, but its makers unwisely decided to take it to pieces in an attempt to improve its performance and reliability, a task that took three days and nights. When it came to the next trial, a freshly cemented boiler joint blew out, scuppering its chances. The field was clear for the *Rocket*, cleverly painted in the fashion of a mail coach to give an impression of speed and lightness.

Rainhill skew bridge, built to carry a road at an angle over the railway. Like the Romans, the designers of the Liverpool to Manchester Railway preferred to build in straight lines. This presented some technical challenges, and engravings of the results were a popular souvenir.

The *Rocket* itself was by no means a perfect engine, but from the moment it chugged up the Rainhill incline, bearing a trainload of directors, it set a pattern for the future. Up until that point, it had been assumed that stationary engines were needed to haul loads up a slope. Now it became clear this was no longer necessarily the case.

Capitalizing on public interest in the trials, the Railway Company offered Rainhill runs to would-be rail travellers in the months leading up to the official opening of the railway on 15 September 1830. One such passenger was Thomas Creevey, who reported in his diary for 14 November 1829:

Today we have had a lark *of a very high order. Lady Wilton sent over yesterday from Knowsley to say that the Loco Motive machine was to be upon the railway at such a place at 12 o'clock for the Knowsley party to ride in if they liked, and inviting this house to be of the party. So of course we were at our post in three carriages and some horsemen at the hour appointed. I had the satisfaction, for I cannot call it* pleasure, *of taking a trip of five miles in it, which we did in just a quarter of an hour – that is 20 miles an hour. As accuracy upon this subject was my great object, I held my watch in my hand at starting, and all the time; and as it had a second hand, I knew I could not be deceived; and it so turned out there was not the difference of a second between the coachee or conductor and myself. But observe, during these five miles, the machine was occasionally made to put itself out or* go it; *and then we went at the rate of 23 miles an hour, and just with the same ease as to motion or absence of friction as the other reduced pace. But the quickest motion is to me* frightful; *it is really flying, and is impossible to divest yourself of the notion of instant death to all upon the least accident happening. It gave me a headache which has not left me yet. …*

The smoke is very inconsiderable indeed, but sparks of fire are abroad in some quantity; one burnt Miss de Ros's cheek, another a hole in Lady Maria's silk pelisse and a third a hole in someone else's gown. Altogether I am extremely glad indeed to have seen this miracle, and to have travelled in it. Had I thought worse of it than I do, I should have had the curiosity to try it; but, having done so, I am quite satisfied with my first *achievement being my* last.

One interesting aspect of this rather Pooterish account is the mention of the ladies, for the railway's directors were particularly keen to encourage female passengers, to overcome a perceived prejudice. Fanny Kemble's rhapsodies at the 'snorting little animal' that flew along the rails were perhaps less typical than her mother's terror on the opening day of the railway: 'I had been unluckily separated from my mother in the first distribution of places, but by an exchange of seats which she was enabled to make she rejoined me when I was at the height of my ecstasy, which was considerably damped by finding that she was frightened to death, and intent upon nothing but devising means of escaping from a situation which appeared to her to threaten with instant annihilation herself and all her travelling companions.'

Prejudice – linked with vested interests – had dogged the early days of planning the Liverpool and Manchester Railway. Some of the objections aired in the House of Commons during discussions around the Act of Parliament that was needed to build the railway were listed in *The History of the English Railway*, by J. A. Francis (1851):

What was to become of the coach-makers and harness-makers, coach-masters, coach-men, inn-keepers, horse-breakers and horse-dealers? The beauty and comfort of country gentlemen's estates would be destroyed by it.

*Was the House aware of the smoke and noise and the hiss which
locomotives passing at ten or twelve miles an hour would [cause]? Iron would
[go up] in price 100 per cent or more or would [run out] altogether. It would be
the greatest nuisance that man could invent. …*

*The country gentleman was told that the smoke would kill the birds as they
passed over the locomotive. The public were told that the weight of the engine
would [stop] it moving; the manufacturer was told that the sparks from its
chimney would burn his goods. Elderly gentlemen were tortured with the [idea]
that they would be run over. Ladies were alarmed at the thought that their
horses would take fright. Cows, it was said, would cease to [give] milk.*

Farmers who faced the loss of their land, and country squires who feared
their view might be spoiled tended to exaggerate their concerns, in the
hopes of gaining large sums in compensation. More immediate were the
worries of the shareholders and owners of canals, and those whose
livelihoods depended upon coach travel. These worries were real.

The whole reason for the establishment of the new railway was to provide
an iron umbilical cord connecting the largest port in Britain with the heart of
its industrial production. Before the railway, getting the raw cotton from
Liverpool to Manchester was not straightforward. From 1760 to 1830, the
trade in cotton had doubled every twenty years. The canals that had been
the transport arteries of the early Industrial Revolution just couldn't keep up
with the demand. Sometimes conveying goods between the cities took more
than twenty-one days, which was longer than the voyage from America to
Liverpool. But from 1830 onwards, the railway was going to speed things up
and whisk tons of the precious cargo from port to loom in a matter of hours.

Once the political decision had been taken to go ahead, there were
practical problems. The new railway crossed some inhospitable territory,
and the fact that surveyors often had to work at night to avoid protesters
did not help. There were bridges, viaducts and embankments to be built,
cuttings to be hacked through rock, and a swamp to be crossed.

The swamp – Chat Moss – had almost proved George Stephenson's undoing in the protracted discussions that had delayed the start of work. In her *Record of a Girlhood*, a besotted Fanny Kemble recalled how she had heard his version of events:

He was a rather stern-featured man, with a dark and deeply marked countenance; his speech was strongly inflected with his native Northumbrian accent, but the fascination of that story told by himself, while his tame dragon flew panting along his iron pathway with us, passed the first reading of the Arabian Nights, *the incidents of which it almost seemed to recall. He was wonderfully condescending and kind in answering all the questions of my eager ignorance, and I listened to him with eyes brimful of warm tears of sympathy and enthusiasm, as he told me of all his alternations of hope and fear, of his many trials and disappointments, related with fine scorn how the 'Parliament men' had badgered and baffled him with their book-knowledge, and how, when at last they thought they had smothered the irrepressible prophecy of his genius in the quaking depths of Chatmoss, he had exclaimed, 'Did ye ever see a boat float on water? I will make my road float upon Chatmoss!' The well-read parliament men (some of whom, perhaps, wished for no railways near their parks and pleasure-grounds) could not believe the miracle, but the shrewd Liverpool merchants, helped to their faith by a great vision of immense gain, did; and so the railroad was made, and I took this memorable ride by the side of its maker, and would not have exchanged the honour and pleasure of it for one of the shares in the speculation.*

The embankment at Chat Moss: 12 square miles of black oozing peat bog which sceptics said could not be crossed. On the surveyor's first visit, he slipped off planks that were being used as a pathway, and had to be dragged out of the treacherous swamp by nearby navvies.

Stephenson's sublime confidence disguised the very real difficulties that had been overcome. Chat Moss was sheer soggy bog, unstable to a depth of 10 to 35 feet, below which was a solid bed of clay. Railway labourers had to strap planks on to their boots, and even horses had to have specially made pattens, to prevent them sinking into the morass. R. H. G. Thomas, in *The Liverpool and Manchester Railway*, describes how at one apparently bottomless pit, Blackpool Hole, contractors tipped spoil solidly for three months without making the slightest progress. Eventually, a nearby plantation of larch trees was cut down, and the trees laid together in a herringbone pattern to form a raft on which to float the foundations of the railway.

Altogether, the final bill for the construction of the railway came to £1,352,950. Given this background, it is understandable that the railway's directors and shareholders should want to make its opening a grand event. Invitations were sent out as early as July, and the guest list – which included four future prime ministers – reads like an 1830 *Who's Who in Politics*. The Prime Minister, the Duke of Wellington, agreed to perform the opening ceremony, and the 'gorgeous car' prepared for such an honoured guest was described in awed tones in the *Liverpool Mercury*:

This carriage was truly magnificent, the sides being beautifully ornamented; superb Grecian scrolls and balustrades, richly gilt, supporting a massy hand-rail all around the carriage, along the whole centre of which was an Ottoman seat for the company. A grand canopy, 24 feet long, was placed aloft upon gilded pillars, so contrived as to be lowered when passing through the tunnel. The drapery was of rich crimson cloth, and the whole surmounted by the ducal coronet. The floor, 32 feet long, by 8 wide, was supported by eight large iron wheels.

One of the Duke's fellow guests was William Huskisson, the MP for Liverpool and a former cabinet minister, who had done much to ease the passage of the Liverpool and Manchester Railway Bill through Parliament. He had often been a lone voice in support of the railway; ironically, he was to pay for his support with his life.

For several days beforehand, the roads into Liverpool had been crowded with sightseers. Entrepreneurs did a fast trade in souvenir jugs, commemorative medals and other knick-knacks. Crowds climbed every suitable building in search of a good viewpoint. The *Manchester Courier* reported that the slates had even been removed from the roof of a dye house near a bridge: 'and a great number of ladies were placed in the attic storey with their heads projecting through the roof – so eager were all to obtain an advantageous view of the procession'. Members of the newly wealthy middle classes paid for seats in specially built grandstands lining the route. The authoress, Mrs M. M. Sherwood, joined a group of a thousand people at Sankey Viaduct – a class-ridden arrangement, as she recalled: 'We got

Commemorative medal showing the 70-foot-high brick and stone viaduct, built to carry the railway over the Sankey canal.

places ... for which we paid three shillings and sixpence each. Though we had to wait some time, we found sufficient occupation for eyes and ears, for there was not a little scolding and gossiping in the broad Lancashire dialect among the ladies who sat near us, and no small elbowing and threatening among the persons below us, who gave their sixpences for a standing.'

Each guest who travelled in the trains was given a list of Orders for the Day before they boarded, to the accompaniment of music from the Wellington Harmonic Band and that of the King's Own Regiment. With the arrival of the Duke of Wellington – the hero of Waterloo – the trumpeters attached to each train played 'See the Conquering Hero Comes'.

ORDERS OF THE DAY.

LIVERPOOL, SEPTEMBER 15th, 1830.

The Directors will meet at the Station, in Crown Street, not later than Nine o'clock in the Morning, and during the assembling of the Company will severally take charge of separate Trains of Carriages to be drawn by the different Engines as follow :—

NORTHUMBRIAN	*Lilac Flag.*	........Mr. MOSS.
PHŒNIX	*Green Flag.*	........Mr. EARLE.
NORTH STAR	*Yellow Flag.*	........Mr. HARRISON.
ROCKET....................	*Light Blue Flag.*	........Mr. A. HODGSON.
DART	*Purple Flag.*	........Mr. SANDARS.
COMET	*Deep Red Flag.*	........Mr. BOURNE.
ARROW	*Pink Flag.*	........Mr. CURRIE.
METEOR.................	*Brown Flag.*	........Mr. DAVID HODGSON.

The men who have the management of the Carriage-breaks will be distinguished by a white ribbon round the arm.

When the Trains of Carriages are attached to their respective Engines a Gun will be fired as a preliminary signal, when the "Northumbrian" will take her place at the head of the Procession ; a second Gun will then be fired, and the whole will move forward.

The Engines will stop at Parkside (a little beyond Newton) to take in a supply of water, during which the company are requested not to leave their Carriages.

At Manchester the Company will alight and remain one hour to partake of the Refreshments which will be provided in the Warehouses at that station. In the farthest warehouse on the right hand side will be the Ladies' Cloak Room.

Before leaving the Refreshment Rooms a Blue Flag will be exhibited as a signal for the Ladies to resume their Cloaks ; after which the Company will repair to their respective Carriages, which will be ranged in the same order as before ; and sufficient time will be allowed for every one to take his seat, according to the number of his Ticket, in the Train to which he belongs; and Ladies and Gentlemen are particularly requested not to part with their Tickets during the day, as it is by the number and colour of the Tickets that they will be enabled at all times to find with facility their respective places in the Procession.

Orders of the Day for the opening ceremony, which was a family affair. As principal engineer, George Stephenson drove the *Northumbrian*. His younger brother drove the *North Star*, and his son, Robert, the *Phoenix*. This notice belonged to Charles Lawrence, the original chairman of the Liverpool and Manchester Railway Company. In his response to Wellington's opening speech, Lawrence said: 'In time to come, this day would be remembered for the spiritual as well as the physical union which was effected between the sister towns of Liverpool and Manchester.' Sadly for him, things turned out differently.

The Duke, directors and other distinguished visitors – issued with special tickets printed in gold on blue-tinted card – travelled in the *Northumbrian*, with seven other trains (including the *Rocket*) following on a parallel line. The *Liverpool Mercury* reported: 'The brilliancy of the cortège, the novelty of the sight, considerations of the almost boundless advantages of the stupendous power about to be put into operation, gave to the spectacle an interest unparalleled – called forth sublime conceptions of the mind and energies of man. On every side the tumultuous voice of praise was heard, and countless hundreds waved their hats to cheer on the sons of enterprise in this their crowning effort.'

However, all was not as well as it seemed. When the gun had been fired to give the signal for the cortège to move off, a bystander had been accidentally injured by a piece of wadding from a cannon, which blew his eye out. The *Manchester Courier* added the gruesome detail that: 'The ball of the eye hung for some time on the cheek, suspended by the integuments!' Worse was to come, when the trains stopped on their parallel lines at Parkside to take on water, and several passengers decided to ignore instructions and get out of the carriages to stretch their legs. What happened next was described in the *Liverpool Mercury* under the headline: MR HUSKISSON'S MOST CALAMITOUS ACCIDENT.

The first fatality. The entry for William Huskisson in the *Dictionary of National Biography* suggests that he was accident-prone, having been lamed by a dislocated ankle, and left with impaired use of an arm after fracturing it three times.

Amongst the number was our Right Hon. Representative; he approached that part at which Mrs Huskisson was sitting, when he caught the eye of the Duke of Wellington. A recognition immediately followed, when the Duke extended his hand, which Mr Huskisson advanced to take. While in the act of shaking hands, herald sounds announced the approach of the Rocket Engine, on the opposite rail: a cry of danger was immediately raised, and Prince Esterhazy was helped into the carriage by Mr Littleton, the Member for Staffordshire. Mr Huskisson remained outside, and several voices exclaimed 'Come in' – 'Take care, Mr Huskisson.' The unfortunate gentleman became flurried, and rapidly caught hold of the door, but, unhappily, in endeavouring to ascend, he missed his footing, and either fell or was thrown down by the door, and on falling to the ground part of his person extended on the other rail, and the Rocket coming up at the instant, went over his leg and thigh, and fractured them in a most dreadful manner. The entire was the work of a moment. An instant previous he was in the full possession of health and spirits, he now lay bleeding and mangled before his friends!

Huskisson, who had had his political differences with the Duke, had clearly seen a good opportunity to make amends but, like the other passengers who so freely wandered across the track, had no conception of the danger he ran. This, coupled with his frailty, led to the accident. George Stephenson and his driver rushed him to a nearby vicarage, breaking the world speed record on the way, but despite the attentions of four surgeons, he had died of his wounds by the end of the day.

Meanwhile, the rest of the party spent more than an hour debating whether or not to go ahead to Manchester. The Duke of Wellington was so shocked that he wanted to abandon the enterprise; others argued that not to complete the inaugural journey would put off potential investors, and disappoint spectators. In the event, some members of the waiting crowd were already angry, as Fanny Kemble reported in her account of what followed:

After this disastrous event the day became overcast, and as we neared Manchester the sky grew cloudy and dark, and it began to rain. The vast concourse of people who had assembled to witness the triumphant arrival of the successful travellers was of the lowest order of mechanics and artisans, among whom great distress and a dangerous spirit of discontent with the Government at that time prevailed. Groans and hisses greeted the carriage, full of influential personages, in which the Duke of Wellington sat. High above the grim and grimy crowd of scowling faces a loom had been erected, at which sat a tattered, starved-looking weaver, evidently set there as a representative man*, to protest against this triumph of machinery, and the gain and glory which the wealthy Liverpool and Manchester men were likely to derive from it. The contrast between our departure from Liverpool and our arrival at Manchester was one of the most striking things I have ever witnessed. The news of Mr Huskisson's fatal accident spread immediately, and his death, which did not occur till the evening, was anticipated by rumour. A terrible cloud covered this great national achievement, and its success, which in every respect was complete, was atoned for to the Nemesis of good fortune by the sacrifice of the first financial statesman of the country.*

Some of the groups of protesters carried the *tricolore*, symbol of the French revolution of 1789, but if they had hoped to emulate the success of the French peasants against their masters they were to be disappointed. Political reform was to come, but no revolution. We will see more clearly the reasons for this as we go back a hundred years in the next chapter.

Meanwhile, despite the ominous accident that cast a shadow over its inauguration, the Liverpool and Manchester Railway flourished. The next morning, the first booked train left Liverpool for Manchester with 140 passengers. The authoress Mrs Sherwood had asked, fearfully: 'Can it be that these terrible Monsters will ever come in to general use?' The answer was a resounding 'yes'.

The enthusiasm of passengers for this new form of transport outstripped all expectations, and other companies were quick to follow the Liverpool and Manchester Railway's example. By 1838 there were 743 miles of track, carrying 5.4 million passengers. In 1842 Queen Victoria made her first journey by steam train from Slough to Paddington, giving respectability to railways. Lines available almost doubled between 1852 and 1870, usage of the railways more than trebled, and the numbers of third-class passengers increased sixfold. By 1871 there were 13,388 miles of track, used by 322.2 million passengers, bringing in £18.1 million in ticket sales.

Equally dramatic was the volume of freight traffic, which had been the original reason for the LMR's existence. The canal companies put up a fight, but in 1850 a train could carry twenty times the amount of a canal barge, and eight times faster, so there was really no competition. Coach companies and turnpikes went bankrupt; in 1846, the last stage-coach left London. Timing is crucial in industrialization. In this case, the iron horse was clearly an idea whose time had come.

Railways changed everyday life. Fast trains meant that fresh fish could be carried further inland, and fish and chips replaced pigs' trotters as a cheap working-class supper. For the first time, poorer people could travel longer distances. Day trips from industrial cities to Blackpool and Scarborough, and from London to the resorts of the south coast became the norm. The first cheap excursion tickets were produced as a result of the huge popularity of the Great Exhibition in 1851 – a good example of the way demand fostered inventive marketing techniques.

On the darker side was the sweated labour of the railway navvies, the tearing up of whole neighbourhoods, and the wild speculation that showed up the worst excesses of the capitalist system.

All that was in the future on that dramatic September day in 1830 but Henry Booth, Administrator and Treasurer of the Liverpool and Manchester Railway, showed his farsightedness with his comments that same year:

We must determine … whether it is desirable that a nation should continue in the quiet enjoyment of pastoral or agricultural life, or that it should be launched into the bustle and excitement of commerce and manufacture. But it must be admitted that the golden age is past and it is to be feared the iron age has succeeded. The locomotive engine and railway were reserved for the present

Passenger carriages on the new Liverpool and Manchester Railway. The *Rocket* colours — yellow and black — were used for first class carriages which also carried mail. Second class passengers travelled in open cattle-truck style carriages.

day. From west to east, and from north to south, the mechanical principle, the philosophy of the nineteenth century, will spread and extend itself. The world has received a new impulse. The genius of the age, like a mighty river of the new world, flows onwards, full, rapid and irresistible.

In that year of change, 1830, not everyone shared Henry Booth's sublime confidence in a bigger and better future. But one thing was certain: things would never be the same again. To understand how Britain had reached this point, we need to turn the clock back a hundred years and move outside this little island.

A View in Whitechapel Road 1830 by Henry Thomas Alken offers a less-than-serious vision of a steam-dominated future.

Chapter Two

WHEELING AND DEALING

100 YEARS

Time: 1730—1830

Place: Meissen—Paris—
Coalbrookdale—
London

Let us strike the key-note, Coketown, before pursuing our tune.

It was a town of red brick, or of brick that would have been red if the smoke and ashes had allowed it; but as matters stood it was a town of unnatural red and black like the painted face of a savage. It was a town of machinery and tall chimneys, out of which interminable serpents of smoke trailed themselves for ever and ever, and never got uncoiled. It had a black canal in it, and a river that ran purple with ill-smelling dye, and vast piles of building full of windows where there was a rattling and a trembling all day long, and where the piston of the steam-engine worked monotonously up and down, like the head of an elephant in a state of melancholy madness. It contained several large streets all very like one another, and many small streets still more like one another, inhabited by people equally like one another, who all went in and out at the same hours, with the same sound upon the same pavements, to do the same work, and to whom every day was the same as yesterday and tomorrow, and every year the counterpart of the last and the next.

These attributes of Coketown were in the main inseparable from the work by which it was sustained; against them were to be set off, comforts of life which found their way all over the world.

CHARLES DICKENS: HARD TIMES (1854)

View over the rooftops of
old Meissen.

The debate about the origins of the Industrial Revolution is a well-worn one. Historians seem unable to agree even when it started, let alone what caused it, although there is a general consensus that it is not enough simply to reel off a list of household names. Of course Hargreaves, Arkwright, Watt and the rest of the crew had their parts to play – but Britain by no means had a monopoly on inventive talent.

Our search for the answer to the riddle began in the age of the *Rocket*: a fairly arbitrary choice, but one that is relatively easy to justify. Britain in 1830 was certainly an exciting place to be – but how, and why, had this happened?

'Of course, you can go through a number of factors and tick them off,' says historian Alan Macfarlane. 'There were advantages economically, it had a very good agricultural system, it had coal. It had advantages religiously, it had Protestantism and free thought. It had political advantages, a reasonable legal framework, a reasonably democratic political system. Yet even when you go through all these, you feel there's something missing, there's an X factor which must have been really special about England and made it different.'

A dispassionate observer of the state of the world in 1730 might have thought that France – then known as the Great Nation – or Germany seemed a much more likely candidate for an industrial revolution.

If you had happened to visit the small German town of Meissen, near Dresden, at this time, you might well have thought something big was about to start there. This was an age when alchemists struggled to find the mystical substance that would turn base metals into noble gold. And in 1730, an alchemist made a discovery that promised to be almost as good: how to make porcelain, or 'white gold' as it was known.

The Chinese, of course, had been making exquisitely crafted porcelain since the eleventh century. Huge amounts of this beautiful but expensive china had been imported to Europe, and extensive efforts had been made to crack the secret of its manufacture. Augustus the Strong, the Elector of Saxony, had his chemists working on it, but it was an alchemist, Johann Friedrich Böttger, who eventually hit on the formula. He discovered that kaolin and petuntse – both to be found in Germany – were the magic ingredients. It took a while to perfect the process, but what happened next was the classic lost opportunity.

While the Chinese had been producing porcelain on a mass scale, selling it to the kings and courts of Europe, the Islamic world and the rest of south-east Asia, Böttger's discovery was used only to satisfy the demand of the court. Chinese porcelain found its way into the homes of the professional and middle classes, as well as the aristocrats. Meissen porcelain remained exclusive, its most typical product the model figurines that replaced the sugar sculptures used to decorate the dessert tables of great banquets. One of the most famous of these, the figure of a tailor sitting on top of a goat, symbolizes perhaps better than anything the rigidity of the court social structure.

The figure was commissioned by Count Brühl, director of the Meissen works, a man with a passion for fine clothes who owned over 300 suits. On one occasion, his tailor had made a particularly fine suit, and Count Brühl exclaimed that he would give him anything he liked. The tailor was cheeky enough to ask for a chance to attend one of the court banquets – an unthinkable prospect for someone so low down in the pecking order. So Count Brühl, amused by this, went to his chief modeller and asked him to do a figure of him.

The result was a figure of the tailor dressed in aristocratic clothing with a finely embroidered silk coat, but mounted on a goat. The tools of his trade – a pair of scissors – were in his hands, while the goat held his iron. So he made it to the table – but only in a grotesque porcelain effigy. History does not relate how he cut Count Brühl's next suit.

Meissen porcelain did not remain the province of the court élite but, even when it became more widely available, it was still prohibitively expensive. Augustus the Strong had jealously guarded the secret of his 'white gold', keeping Böttger locked away in his castle to prevent communication with the outside world. Production carried on in traditional ways, and there was little sense of the possibilities offered by a wider market. In England, by contrast, manufacturers like Wedgwood were constantly in touch with the buying public. He could provide a dinner service for the Empress of Russia as easily as the china for a middle-class tea party. He knew what he wanted – and, by imaginative marketing, he could

Jacques de Vaucanson, inventor extraordinaire, astonishes his servant with his mechanical flute player. On a pedestal to his left is the digesting duck. Lithograph by Albert Chereau.

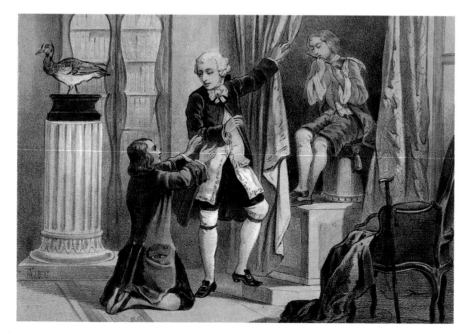

persuade large numbers of people that they wanted the same thing. As we will see, the story of Wedgwood neatly illustrates the comment made by Charles, Marquis de Biencourt: 'The English have the wit to make things for the people, rather than for the rich.'

So, on the evidence of Meissen, at least, it seems that a single discovery of a technique does not on its own lead to an industrial revolution. Perhaps the secret lies in mass production? If a machine could reliably reproduce the actions of man, then perhaps it could reduce the cost of manufacture. Many people across Europe were experimenting in this area in the early eighteenth century – and some of the most ingenious devices were being made in France. One of Simon Schaffer's favourite examples is Vaucanson's automatic digesting duck, produced in 1731.

'Jacques de Vaucanson was a bright young man from south-eastern France, who grew up near the Alps and was trained by men of the Church to build ingenious little clockwork devices,' explains Simon Schaffer. 'He left home when he was very young – he had got into trouble with his teachers and his family – and he came to Paris. His career in early-eighteenth-century Paris tells us a great deal about what was possible, and what was not, in France as opposed to England.

'What he did when he was in Paris was to make his name when he was in his twenties by building three automata – machines that mimic the behaviour of living beings. They would have been very familiar in market squares, on churches, in fairgrounds. What was unusual about Vaucanson's machines was their extraordinary technical skill. He designed a machine that was a drummer, one which was a flute player, and, above all, his famous duck. This was a machine in the shape and size of a normal duck, that could apparently do the things a normal duck could do. It could flap its wings, lift and open its beak, it could defecate … it was terribly impressive. It was put on show at the big Paris fairs. It was shown to the King. It stayed the image of what eighteenth-century ingenuity is all about to such an extent that there is a man at the moment who is in fact building a working precise replica of Vaucanson's duck.'

The replica is being created for a private collection by David Secrett, who is trained as an organ builder. With little but guesswork to go on for some parts of the mechanism, the process of creating it has clearly shown the extent of Vaucanson's inventiveness. Like the original 'digesting duck', the replica displays its wings, spreads its tail feathers and feeds from a bowl, but the final part of the cycle has proved trickier. Vaucanson had worked on machines to illustrate medical theories, including an attempt at building an *anatomie mouvante* to show that digestion was a chemical process, rather than a purely mechanical one in which food is broken up. Original accounts of the duck's 'digestion' process suggest that it was accompanied by a very realistic smell. So how did Vaucanson achieve this?

'I think he eventually reconciled himself to the fact that he was just not going to be able to put a chemistry lab inside this machine, which is what he would have had to do,' says Simon Schaffer. 'So one of the problems in understanding what Vaucanson was up to is the story about how the duck eats and defecates. There's this great debate about whether the duck was a trick in that sense, that it ingests food at one end and then you synchronize defecation at the other, and there's nothing chemical going on inside at all.'

Whatever the truth of the matter, there is no doubt about the inventiveness involved. However, ingenuity on its own was not enough – as was demonstrated when Vaucanson tried to apply his talents to the wider field of the French silk industry in the 1740s and 1750s.

'When he had made quite a pile of money as showman, entrepreneur, technician, he was hired by the French government to do to the French silk trade what the Europeans had been trying to do to China's porcelain trade,' says Simon Schaffer. 'Vaucanson, as engineer, was given the job by the French government of designing and then setting up a completely new kind of silk mill, based on a rather dramatically automated set of machines to spin and weave silk. He was given military backing, he was given finance, he was given a State monopoly.

'He moved to the great French city of Lyon, which was the Birmingham of France, and tried to set up his silk works there. There was massive protest from silk workers, from the existing silk bosses. He had to get out of town in a hurry. He managed to escape at night, dressed as a monk. His mill was burnt down, his machines were broken, State support was withdrawn.

'Towards the end of his life – the 1760s and 1770s – he set up a few silk factories in the area of Ardèche on enlightened rational lines, as he saw it, with machines that were obviously going to throw lots of people out of work and make silk in relatively large quantities.'

The reason for the difficulties encountered by both of these schemes, according to Simon Schaffer, was the 'top down' model of French industrial development.

'The initiatives I have just talked about are from Paris, they come from the government, from the Board of Trade, from the Bureau of Commerce; they are imposed on the great French provincial centres by the capital. What you see is a rational, planned, absolutely sensible and in the end rather ineffective system of automation and industrial change.'

In eighteenth-century England, by contrast, many initiatives came from local response to local demand, and succeeded because of the business talent of individual entrepreneurs. Some of the best-known names associated with the Industrial Revolution in England are remembered not so much for their inventions, as for what they did with them. Typical is Richard Arkwright, the one-time barber and wig-maker who is generally credited in history books with making the step from hand to water power in cotton spinning. His water frame, patented in 1769, used pairs of rollers to replace the human finger and thumb in the spinning process. In fact, the technical genius behind this idea was his collaborator, John Kay, a Warrington clock-maker. Arkwright's contribution was in its marketing.

The secret of his success was simple. Determined to make the most of the invention before his patents ran out, he would sell his water frames only in units of 1,000. This not only made him huge profits – it effectively forced others into operating on the same scale as his own successful water-driven mill at Cromford, where he employed 600 workers, most of them children. He is thus credited by many as being effectively the inventor of the factory system in Britain. He may have developed the idea initially for his own benefit – but he ensured its spread.

Portrait of a well-fed capitalist: Sir Richard Arkwright, whose marketing methods led to the spread of the factory system.

Judging by contemporary accounts, he was also an effective self-publicist. He was knighted in 1786, made Lord Lieutenant of Derby in the following year, and clearly made the most of the opportunities this offered for self-aggrandizement. The *Manchester Mercury* for 27 March 1787 noted: 'On Sunday last, Sir Richard Arkwright … arrived at Derby, accompanied by a number of gentlemen, etc., on horseback, his javelin men thirty in number, exclusive of bailiffs, dressed in the richest liveries ever seen there on such an occasion. They all rode on black horses. The trumpeters were mounted on grey horses, and elegantly dressed in scarlet and gold.'

Andrew Ure, the arch apologist for industry, gives an oleaginous description of Arkwright's contribution in *The Philosophy of the Manufacturers* (1835):

When the first water-frames for spinning cotton were erected at Cromford, in the romantic valley of the Derwent, about sixty years ago, mankind were little aware of the mighty revolution which the new system of labour was destined by Providence to achieve, not only in the structure of British society, but in the fortunes of the world at large. Arkwright alone had the sagacity to discern, and the boldness to predict in glowing language, how vastly productive human industry would become, when no longer proportioned in its results to muscular effort, which is by its nature fitful and capricious, but when made to consist in the task of guiding the work of mechanical fingers and arms, regularly impelled with great velocity by some indefatigable physical power.

Joseph Wright of Derby painted a romanticized picture of Cromford Mill, nestling in a valley at sunset. However, he also painted a rather less romantic portrait of its owner, now hanging in the office of the Director of the Science Museum in London. This clearly shows Arkwright's ruthlessness and determination – a determination which meant that when he died, in 1792, he was worth half a million pounds.

If Arkwright is cast in many people's minds as the typical heartless capitalist, there were other manufacturers with a social conscience. The contribution of the Dissenters – Quakers, Methodists, Baptists and Congregationalists – to the Industrial Revolution in Britain has been well documented. Kept out of Establishment public life by their religion, many found outlets for their talents in trade and commerce. As Asa Briggs put it in *The Age of Improvement*: 'Their religious solidarity, symbolized in Quaker meeting house or non-conformist chapel, facilitated not only consciousness of Grace but confident mutual borrowing and lending. Reliance on the Good Book and on keeping good books went together.'

A good illustration of this influence comes in Coalbrookdale, that darkly dramatic site on the banks of the River Severn where iron and coal came together in a unique way that pointed towards an industrial future.

Many contemporary accounts survive describing the dramatic growth of this one-time village. Typical is the prospectus written to accompany two engravings which are the earliest published views of Coalbrookdale. The author, George Perry, lived in Coalbrookdale and was the principal partner in an iron works there.

In the year One Thousand Seven Hundred, the whole Village consisted of only One furnace, Five Dwelling Houses, and a Forge or two. About Forty years ago the present Iron-foundry was establish'd, and since that time its Trade and Buildings are so far increas'd that it contains at least Four Hundred and Fifty inhabitants, and finds employment for more than Five Hundred People, including all the several Occupations that are connected with the Works. ...

THIS place affords a number of delightful prospects. One might venture to say that all the Principal Beauties of landscape may be observ'd from some or other of the Hills that surround it. Some of the Hills are cover'd with Verdure, others overgrown with Wood, and some again are naked and barren. These, with a View of a fine fertile Country, Water'd by the Severn, all contribute to form as agreeable a Variety to the Eye, as can well be conceiv'd. The Beauty of the scene is in the meantime greatly increas'd by a new view of the Dale itself. Pillars of Flame and smoke rising to vast height, large Reservoirs of Water, and a number of Engines in motion, never fail to raise the admiration of strangers, tho' it must be confess'd these things join'd to the murmuring of the Waterfalls, the noise of the Machines, and the roaring of the Furnaces, are apt to occasion a kind of Horror in those who happen to arrive in a dark Night. UPON the whole, there are perhaps few Places where rural prospects, and Scenes of hurry and Business are so happily united as at COALBROOKDALE.

The story of Coalbrookdale is partly the story of the Darby family, who were industrious Quakers. Abraham Darby had been making brass cooking pots down in Bristol, and had been working on a way of smelting iron using coke. He thought that if he could make large amounts of cast iron he could make more pots and more money. As it happened, other members of his family were already using coke furnaces in Shropshire. He used his connections, and moved to Coalbrookdale to start making pots in factory quantities.

John Challen, an iron expert based at Coalbrookdale, explains Darby's thinking. 'Being a brass-maker turning to iron, he naturally thought well, if it worked for brass, it'll work for iron,' he says. 'And so he came here with the intention of using the local coal: the Shropshire coal field was one of the biggest coal fields in Europe at the time, so there was plenty of coal. There was an out-of-work blast furnace just up from a brass works which the Quakers had in the bottom of Coalbrookdale, so it was a good opportunity. He took over the furnace, repaired it, and almost straight away started experimenting with the local coals. The point being that instead of using the coal raw, he was burning out all the impurities, getting a very pure source of carbon. That's what he was using in the furnace, and in 1709 he successfully smelted his first iron using coke, just to make cast-iron pots.

A View of the Upper Works at Coalbrook Dale, an engraving based on a drawing by George Perry, whose accompanying prospectus gave a glowing description of the area. In the foreground, a team of horses pull a newly cast cylinder for a steam engine. To the right there are steaming piles of coke.

'The reason it all got going then, of course, is there were early railways here, wooden railways, the mines were getting deeper, so there were all sorts of new uses. People were soon knocking on the door of the iron works, saying, "Well, if you can cast iron pots, can you make me some iron wheels? Can you make us cylinders for the steam engines? Can you make us rails?" And you started to get all these new innovations for using this wonderful material, cast iron.

The Iron Bridge, Coalbrookdale by William Williams, 1780. Abraham Darby III paid Williams ten guineas for this view of the bridge, which became the high spot of many sightseeing tours. In the centre, two elegantly dressed ladies are being shown its finer points from a boat.

'Up until that stage the traditional iron industry had all been focused on wrought iron, which is the iron that the blacksmiths use, but cast iron is, if you like, the plastic of the age. You could pour it, you could shape it, you could use it to mass-produce quite simple objects. And this is how Coalbrook started to make its name.'

The first cast-iron cylinders for steam engines, produced at Coalbrookdale in the 1720s, were one of the things that made the steam engine more affordable. And, of course, the vast iron bridge that today gives the area its popular name was the best possible advertisement for cast iron. Contemporary accounts unite in their admiration of its breathtaking scale. Typical is this diary entry by Samuel Butler, a Warwickshire gentleman not to be confused with the author of the same name (although they were related). In his entry for Friday 14 March 1782 he wrote:

There was formerly no other passage across the Severn in the Dale than by a ferry but in the year 1775 or 76 a plan was projected for throwing a Cast Iron Bridge over of such a construction as to admit Vessels to pass under it without lowering the Mast – this project was accordingly pursued and compleated under the direction of a Mr Darby – a Gentleman greatly concern'd in the Iron works carried on in the said Dale – the expence of this undertaking is said to have been 5000 Guineas. The Bridge itself makes a light & elegant appearance tho' apparently no ways deficient in Strength. In viewing it either up or down water it resembles an elegant Arch in some ancient Cathedral … whilst viewing the Bridge a loaded Vessell pass'd under it & tho' they said the River was then 4 feet higher than low water mark, yet the Bridge appear'd to be many feet above the top of the Mast.

The River Severn – providing a ready water supply, as well as transport – was a crucial factor in the success of the area. George Perry, writing in the *Gentleman's Magazine*, noted:

This river, being justly esteemed the second in Britain, is of great importance on account of its trade, being navigated by vessels of large burden more than 160 miles from the sea, without the assistance of any lock; upwards of 100,000 tons of coals are annually shipped from the collieries about Broseley and Madeley to the towns situated on its banks, and from thence into the adjacent countries: also great quantities of grain, pig and bar iron, iron manufactures and earthenwares; as well as wool, hops, cyder and provisions, are constantly exported to Bristol and other places, from whence merchants' goods are brought in return.

Visitors came to view the spectacle, with mixed reactions. Arthur Young, the agricultural journalist, noted in a diary entry for 13 June 1776:

Viewed the furnaces, forges, etc. with the vast bellows that give those roaring blasts, which make the whole edifice horribly sublime. These works are supposed to be the greatest in England. The whole process is here gone through from digging the iron stone to making it into cannons, pipes, cylinders, etc. etc. All the iron used is raised in the neighbouring hills, and the coal dug likewise. … Mr Darby in his works employs near 1,000 people, including colliers. There are 5 furnaces in the Dale, and 2 of them are his.

These iron works are in a very flourishing situation, rising rather than the contrary. Coalbrook Dale itself is a very romantic spot, it is a winding glen between two immense hills which break into various forms, and all thickly covered with wood, forming the most beautiful sheets of hanging wood. Indeed too beautiful to be much in unison with that variety of horrors art has spread at the bottom: the noise of the forges, mills, &c with all their vast machinery, the flames bursting from the furnaces with the burning of the coal and the smoak of the lime kilns, are altogether sublime.

A decade after Arthur Young's account, digging to make an underground canal to reach the coalmines had uncovered a spring of natural bitumen which became known as the Tar Tunnel. An Italian aristocrat, Carlo Castone della Torre di Renzionico Comasco, who visited in 1787, was transfixed by what he described as a 'fountain of liquid pitch': 'At length we arrived at the rock whence emerges the pitchy torrent in such copiousness that five or six barrels are filled with it every day. The workmen who gather the pitch are, of a truth, like the imps described by Dante in his *Inferno* as gathering with a hook the souls of the damned into a lake of pitch – so horribly disfigured and begrimed are they.'

The actor Charles Dibdin similarly employed the vocabulary of hell to describe his visit in the same year. His account gives a clear idea of what working conditions must have been like.

It was our intention, I remember, to stay all the night, but this was impossible, for the day was insufferably hot, and the prodigious piles of coal burning to coke, the furnaces, the forges, and the other tremendous objects emitting fire and smoke to an immense extent, together with the intolerable stench of the sulphur, approached very nearly to the idea of being placed in an air pump. We were glad enough to get away and sleep at Shifnal. …

Coalbrookdale by Night by Philippe Jacques de Loutherbourg, 1801. De Loutherbourg started his artistic career as a designer and painter of stage sets, hence the theatrical nature of this dramatic depiction of the Bedlam Furnaces, downstream from the Iron Bridge.

Coalbrookdale wants nothing but Cerberus to give you an idea of the heathen hell. The Severn may pass for the Styx, with this difference that Charon, turned turnpike man, ushers you over the bridge instead of rowing in his crazy boat; the men and women might easily be mistaken for devils and fairies, and the entrance of any one of these blazing caverns where they polish the cylinders, for Tartarus; and, really, if any atheist who had never heard of Coalbrookdale, could be transported there in a dream, and left to awake at the mouth of one of those furnaces, surrounded on all sides by such a number of infernal objects, though he had been all his life the most profligate unbeliever that ever added blasphemy to incredulity, he would infallibly tremble at the last judgement that in imagination would appear to him.

Abraham Darby succeeded at Coalbrookdale because he was in the right place at the right time. But historical accident is only part of the story. The other part is the X factor with which this chapter started. Alan Macfarlane has a theory about what this might be.

'If you are going to have an industrial or scientific revolution which is immensely complex, you need a kind of social organization which will encourage a blend of two things. On the one hand you need individuals who are thinking hard, trying hard, competing. On the other, you need co-operation, collaboration, trust and mutual solidarity, so that the ideas can be shared and generated together. This is a very difficult thing to do in most societies – there's either too much individualism or too much cooperation and everything is dead. What the English developed, and has now spread over much of the world, was a way of bringing these together.'

Abraham Darby's factory was not government funded or approved (unlike Vaucanson's silk enterprise in France). He made use of the network of his Quaker family, used their pre-existing furnaces to smelt his iron, and plugged into a market that he already knew. He then set up a trust – that fundamental bulwark of eighteenth-century networking to run the whole enterprise. The trust, an association of people who came together to hold wealth jointly rather than as individuals, was the basis of the Coalbrookdale Company, the Stock Exchange and the Bank of England.

The coffee house, which grew in popularity throughout the eighteenth century, provided a marvellous informal meeting place. A visiting French-man, the Abbé Prevost, was particularly impressed at the way these institutions crossed class boundaries. He wrote:

I have had pointed out to me in several coffee houses a couple of lords, a baronet, a shoemaker, a tailor, a wine-merchant, and some others of the same sort, all sitting round the same table and discussing familiarly the news of the court and town. The government's affairs are as much the concern of the people as of the great. Every man has the right to discuss them freely. Men condemn, approve, revile, rail with bitter invectives both in speech and in writing without the authorities daring to intervene. The King himself is not secure from censure. The coffee houses and other public places are the seats of English liberty. For two pence you have the right to read all the papers for and against the government and to take a cup of tea or coffee as well.

Perhaps the best-known frequenters of coffee houses were literary figures such as Samuel Johnson. But the coffee houses were also the catalyst for the establishment of such famous institutions as the Stock Exchange and Lloyd's insurance (which originated in Lloyd's Coffee House, where people went to get all the shipping news).

Gradually, those in the higher echelons of society took themselves off to gentlemen's clubs. And the growth of these, and clubs of all kinds, is a crucial part of the X factor that explains the Industrial Revolution in Britain, according to Alan Macfarlane.

'We now live in a world which has millions of clubs and we all take it for granted that this is the kind of thing humans can do,' he says. 'But in most civilizations, clubs have been a political threat to the State; because they often encourage free thinking, they've been a threat to the Church, and so they have been banned or people have had their primary loyalties to their family or to their village.'

Networking eighteenth-century style – in a coffee house.

In France, for instance, clubs were banned. But eighteenth- and nineteenth-century Britain saw the heyday of clubs – many of which still survive. These provided a highly structured and controlled social framework for a new way of doing things.

'It's just like a group of children really, but they meet regularly, often in a building which they've bought. They have club rules, they have club finances, they have a committee to run it. And above all, they take a lot of care about who are members,' says Professor Macfarlane. 'This gives a great sense of loyalty and commitment. The club has a kind of wall round it, it's difficult to get in, it has this building, it has rituals, it has pictures on the wall, it has deferential servants who say, "Good morning, sir" etc., etc. So you come in and you unwind and relax with people who have chosen you and you have chosen.

'It's only when you can get separate individuals with all their skills, all their different backgrounds, to come together trustingly, to work together and to share their knowledge and information and skills, that you can build something as complex as an industrial civilization. One person can't do it: ten people can't do it. You need all the accumulated skills of writers, academics, politicians, businessmen, craftsmen, put together to make this new kind of civilization. And the British club made this possible.'

There were all sorts of clubs in eighteenth-century Britain, but – according to Alan Macfarlane – the one which represents best the connection between clubs and science and industry was the bizarrely named Lunar Society, based in Birmingham.

'This was founded by Darwin's grandfather, Erasmus Darwin, and it used to meet once a month on the full moon for six hours, from two o'clock until eight o'clock. And people would sit round and have a kind of seminar on some topic of current interest. The seminars would have been fascinating: they were given by some of the greatest inventors and industrialists of the eighteenth century.

'For instance, Josiah Wedgwood the potter would talk about problems in pottery, to which Joseph Priestley, the chemist, would offer his solutions. Or again, James Watt, the inventor of the modern steam engine, would be there, and he would talk about problems with the steam engine and how you were going to distribute it and make it. And Matthew Boulton, the greatest eighteenth-century ironmaster, was a member of the society. He'd say, "Well, why don't we go into partnership, then?"'

Professor Macfarlane's favourite illustration of the Lunar Society's unique mixture of enthusiasm, curiosity, trust and tolerance is the story of the snake. This is retold in the autobiography of Mary Anne Schimmel Penninck, the daughter of a society member.

To this society … belonged the celebrated Dr Withering, distinguished alike in botany and medicine; and of whom it was said, years afterwards, when his life was terminating by a lingering consumption, 'The Flower of Physic is indeed Withering.' Then came Dr Stoke, profoundly scientific and eminently absent. On one occasion, when the Lunar meeting, or 'Lunatics', as our butler called them, were seated at dinner, a blazing fire being in the room, we were astonished by hearing a sudden hissing noise, and seeing a large and beautiful yellow and black snake rushing about the room. My dear mother, who saw it was not venomous, said to me: 'Mary Anne, go and catch that snake;' which, after some trouble … I succeeded in accomplishing. We were wondering where it could have come from, when Dr Stoke said that, as he was riding along, he had seen the poor animal frozen on a bank, and put it in his pocket to dissect, but the snake had thawed, and escaped from his pocket. The doctor praised me very much for my prowess in the capture of the snake, and as a reward, he made me a present of my prisoner, which I long kept in a glass jar, and carefully tended every day; at last, however, I gave him his freedom.

Slightly less eccentric were organizations such as the Manchester Literary and Philosophical Society, founded in 1781 and still going strong. Most of the original members were physicians, surgeons or apothecaries but they were later joined by merchants, engineers and manufacturers. The objects of the Lit and Phil, as it is popularly known, are: 'to promote the education and the widening of public interest in, and appreciation of, any form of literature, science, the arts and public affairs, provided that no activity involving party politics or controversial theology shall be included in the pursuit of these objects'. The society's memoirs, covering two centuries of lectures and meetings, have an author and subject index with almost 12,000 entries.

In the middle of the seventeenth century, when the scientific revolution was in full swing, it had centred on the Royal Society in London. By the end of the eighteenth century it was largely a provincial movement. If Manchester had its philosophical society, so too did Norwich, Northampton, Exeter, Bristol, Bath, Plymouth, Derby and Newcastle.

A much-quoted example of the way group dynamics can foster invention is the story of Edmund Cartwright and the power loom, which may or may not be apocryphal.

'Cartwright, who was an Oxford don and local clergyman in the Midlands, was having dinner with a group of local industrialists in 1784,' Simon Schaffer explains. 'Their problem was just this: they could make thread very, very fast and in large quantities, but they had a block at the process of weaving. As weaving was certainly not automated, but done on hand looms still, their problem was that they could supply far more thread to weavers than weavers could then process rapidly. Cartwright had heard about a machine which was on show in London in 1784, an automaton which could play chess and win. It was in the shape of a Turk, because all exotic things came from the East, and Cartwright had read about this in the newspaper – he may even have seen it, because it was on tour. He said, "If people are clever enough to build a machine which can play and win at chess, surely we can build a machine which can weave cloth?"'

In fact, later observers revealed the 'automaton' as a fraud, but Cartwright's inspiration helped industry to make the leap forward it required. The story also neatly illustrates the way the field of invention was open to anyone, whatever their speciality or social background. The cosy world of clubs, philosophical societies and middle-class dinner tables is only part of the story.

James Hargreaves, who had invented the spinning jenny in 1764, was a humble weaver and carpenter from Blackburn. His spinning machine was named after his wife, whom he had watched working at her wheel, and it enabled women to spin up to eighty threads at once, as opposed to six or seven. Richard Arkwright, originally a barber and wig-maker, got the idea for his water frame while travelling around Nottinghamshire and

Derbyshire, collecting human hair for wigs. But the best-known example of an inventor who started from humble beginnings is James Watt.

Perhaps because of the romantic schoolboy picture of Watt sitting in his mother's kitchen watching a kettle boil, it is widely assumed that the steam engine was entirely Watt's idea. In fact, the first steam engine was built by Thomas Newcomen in 1712, and was used to pump water out of a Cornish tin mine. Watt's contribution was to make crucial improvements that greatly increased the efficiency of the design, saving fuel, and enabling it to be used almost anywhere.

Born in 1736 in Greenock, Scotland, Watt had gone to London at the age of nineteen to learn instrument-making. Ill health forced him to return home to Scotland, and he went to work as an instrument-maker in the University of Glasgow. In 1764, he was given a model of Thomas Newcomen's engine to repair. He saw its faults, and began to work on a better model.

The story goes that inspiration struck while he was out on a Sunday stroll. The solution, he decided, was to have a separate condenser which would remain permanently cool, while the piston cylinder was kept permanently hot. The very next day he successfully experimented with a borrowed brass syringe and a tin can. In *A Narrative of Mr Watt's Invention of the Improved Engine*, written several years afterwards, Professor John Robison described Watt's taciturn satisfaction at his success:

Romanticized picture showing James Watt deep in thought over a boiling kettle. He made vital improvements to steam-engine design, and was the originator (with his partner, Matthew Boulton) of the term 'horse power'.

I came into Mr Watt's parlour without ceremony, and found him sitting before the fire, having lying on his knee a little tin cistern, which he was looking at. I entered into conversation on what we had been speaking of at our last meeting – something about steam. All the while, Mr Watt kept looking at the fire, and laid down the cistern at the foot of his chair. At last he looked at me, and said briskly, 'You need not fash yourself any more about that, man; I have now got an engine that shall not waste a particle of steam. It shall be all boiling hot; – aye, and hot water injected if I please.' So saying, Mr Watt looked with complacency at the little thing at his feet, and, seeing that I observed him, he shoved it away under a table with his foot. I put a question to him about the nature of his contrivance. He answered me rather drily. I did not press him to a further explanation at that time, knowing that I had offended him a few days before by blabbing a pretty contrivance which he had hit on for turning the cocks of the engine. I had mentioned this in the presence of an engine-builder who was going to erect one for a friend of mine, and this having come to Mr Watt's ears, he found fault with it.

Watt eventually left Scotland for Birmingham in 1775, and went into partnership with Matthew Boulton to manufacture steam engines. It is estimated that close to 2,500 steam engines were built in the eighteenth century, of which about 30 per cent were made by Watt.

In his book *The Lever of Riches*, Joel Mokyr gives Watt as a typical example of the kind of human power behind the Industrial Revolution:

Watt's work, which combined inventive genius with a desire to cut costs, minimize wear and tear, and extract the last drop of duty from the last puff of steam in his engine was paradigmatic of the kind of mind that helped make the Industrial Revolution.

Watt himself, in his oddly written third-person autobiography, wrote that 'his mind ran upon making engines cheap as well as good'. The search for economic value in addition to functionality and beauty represents the culmination of a millennium of development of European technological rationality. Yet rationality meant nothing without technical ability, and Watt's mechanical talents bordered on the virtuoso. In short, in the history of power technology, Watt is comparable to, say, Pasteur in biology, Newton in physics, or Beethoven in music. Some individuals did matter.

Watt's phrase 'cheap as well as good' hints at an essential element in attempting to make sense of the puzzle that is the Industrial Revolution in Britain: the profit motive.

'The presumption in Britain was first and foremost that an innovation was supposed to make money, it was supposed to be commercialized,' says Joel Mokyr. 'Nobody is averse to money in any society that I know of, but in France innovations were first and foremost supposed to serve the State. They were geared towards the military, and what was not useful for the military could be used to entertain the upper class. There you have Vaucanson's duck, and so on.'

He argues that, in Britain, the popularity of public lectures about scientific inventions was simply because people thought that somewhere, something could be said that could help them to make money.

A key feature of the eighteenth century, which is often suggested as one of the causes of the Industrial Revolution, was a steadily rising population. Britain's population almost doubled, with a particularly marked growth towards the end of the century. Of course, the population was still tiny by today's standards. (One historian has suggested that the best way of visualizing this is to remove six out of seven

Portrait of Josiah Wedgwood by Sir Joshua Reynolds, 1782. Wedgwood and Watt both had a sense of the importance of partnership for a successful business. While Watt had his Boulton, Wedgwood had his Bentley.

people in our current population.) But more people in society meant more people to man factories, and more people to sell to. This opened up the possibility of a mass market.

Daniel Defoe described eighteenth-century Britain as consisting of two classes of people: manufacturers and shopkeepers. Most popular histories of the Industrial Revolution concentrate on the manufacturers, but the birth of consumerism is equally important. One figure who straddles both worlds like a Colossus is that of Josiah Wedgwood. He had the instincts of a scientist, carrying out over 5,000 meticulously recorded experiments which produced his distinctive Jasper Ware, as well as the first pyrometer (developed to measure the temperature inside his pottery kilns). He had the organizational drive needed for successful manufacturing, producing fine pottery in quantities that made it affordable to those he termed 'the middling classes'. But the real reason Wedgwood is still a name to conjure with today is because of his early incursions into that territory we tend perhaps to think of as exclusively twentieth-century: the creation of a designer label.

Born in Burslem, Staffordshire, in 1730, Josiah Wedgwood was the youngest of the thirteen children of Thomas and Mary Wedgwood of the Churchyard Pottery. After serving his apprenticeship, he was taken into partnership in 1754 by Thomas Whieldon of Fenton, the greatest English potter of his time. He then began his experiments, as he wrote in his Experiment Book: 'To try for some more solid improvement, as well in the *Body*, as the *Glazes*, the *Colours*, and the *Form* of the articles of our manufacture.'

In 1759 he set up his own business by renting a small pottery, the Ivy House Works, for £15 a year and employing his cousin as a journeyman. He prospered, moving in 1762 to the larger 'Bell' Works, so named from his habit of summoning his workers by bell instead of the usual horn. In the same year he met the Liverpool merchant, Thomas Bentley, with whom he was to form a close partnership. His letters to Bentley – rescued in the mid nineteenth century from a scrap merchant's yard, where they were being sold to local grocers as wrapping paper – show clearly how carefully he calculated the marketing of his products.

This newspaper advertisement for Wedgwood's Queen's Ware shows how Wedgwood extracted maximum publicity value from his royal commission.

QUEEN's WARE and ORNAMENTAL VASES, manufactured by Josiah Wedgwood, Potter to her Majesty, are sold at his Warehouse, the Queen's Arms, the Corner of Great Newport Street, Long Acre, where, and at his Works at Burslim in Staffordshire, Orders are executed on the shortest Notice.

As he now sells for ready Money only, he delivers the Goods safe, and Carriage free to London.

☞ His Manufacture stands the Lamp for Stewing, &c. without any Danger of breaking, and is sold at no other Place in Town.

An early success came with his development of fine, cheap, cream-coloured earthenware. In 1765 he supplied Queen Charlotte with a complete set of creamware tea things – and, with royal consent, cannily renamed the product Queen's Ware. In 1767 he wrote with disarming frankness in a letter to Bentley: 'The demand for this sd. Creamcolour, Alias Queen's Ware, Alias Ivory still increases. – It is really amazing how rapidly the use of it has spread almost over the whole Globe, & how universally it is liked – How much of this general use, & estimation, is owing to the mode of its introduction – & how much to its real utility & beauty? are questions in which we may be a good deal interested for the governmt of our future Conduct.'

Wedgwood and Bentley's success in royal circles, following Wedgwood's appointment as Potter to the Queen, is underlined in one of Bentley's rare surviving letters, written to a friend in Liverpool: 'Mr Wedgwood and I had a long audience of their majesties at the Queen's palace to present some bas-reliefs her majesty had ordered; and to show some new improvements with which they were well pleased. They expressed in the most obliging and condescending manner, their attention to our manufacture and entered very freely into conversation on the further improvement of it, and on many other subjects.'

Wedgwood's most famous commission in Queen's Ware was a 952-piece dinner and dessert service for Empress Catherine II of Russia, which featured freehand paintings of 1,244 different English scenes. This was known as the Frog Service, because each piece bore a frog crest. It was a risky enterprise for Wedgwood. He realized that the cost and difficulty of painting so many individual scenes might chip away at his profit margins, but at the same time he also realized its potential advertisement value. His solution was to capitalize on the fashionable enthusiasm for exhibitions by putting the Empress' china on show in London. Admission to the exhibition was by ticket only, thus adding to its exclusive air.

Wedgwood built a splendid factory near Newcastle-under-Lyme, which he named Etruria, after the area in central Italy where archaeologists had found many fine pots. (It seems to have been a word that he had heard before he saw it written, for it made its first appearance in his letters as 'Hetruria'.) He constructed a village for his workers, improved roads and raised money for the canal system which brought prosperity to the Staffordshire potteries. Symbolically, he cut the first sod of earth to start construction of the Trent and Mersey Canal in 1766. His house, Etruria Hall, faced the canal and his factory, illustrating his pride in his achievements.

He introduced the idea of the travelling salesman, and had many promotions aimed at the provinces. He offered free carriage of his goods anywhere in the country, a money-back guarantee for dissatisfied customers, and free replacement for breakages. But he always realized the central importance of a London base. In the early days, his brother John acted as his agent. But as business increased, he realized that more was needed. On 2 August 1765 he wrote to John: 'You know I have often mention'd having a man in London the greatest part of the year, shewing patterns, takeing orders, settleing accounts etc etc & as I increase my work, & throw it more in the ornamental way I shall have the greatest need of such assistance & should be glad to have your advice upon it. Would £50 a year keep such a Person in London & pay rent for 2 Rooms?'

London's size made it the single most important market, as it housed about 11 per cent of the population of mid eighteenth-century England. It was also the distribution centre, as middlemen tended to buy their stock from London china and pottery dealers rather than direct from the manufacturers. But, most importantly for Wedgwood, it was the centre of fashion. Once he had opened his London showroom, this and his association with royalty and nobility ensured his high social standing.

Wedgwood's partner, Thomas Bentley. He is pictured with some of the Jasper Ware that made the Wedgwood name famous.

Wedgwood had a keen sense of his market, and took great care of the needs of his (mostly female) customers. It is interesting to note his coy use of euphemisms for the business of selling in this letter to Thomas Bentley of 31 May 1767:

I find I did not sufficiently explain to you my reasons for wanting a large Room. It was not to shew or have a large stock of Ware in town, but to enable me to shew various Table and desert services, completely set out on two ranges of Tables … in order to do the needfull with the ladys in the neatest, genteelest and best method. The same, or indeed a much greater variety of setts of vases should decorate the Walls, and both these articles may, every few days, be so alter'd, revers'd & transform'd as to render the whole a new scene, even to the same company, every time they shall bring their friends to visit us. I need not tell you the very good effects this must produce, when business and pleasure can be made to go hand in hand. Every new show, Exhibition, or variety soon grows stale in London, & is no longer

regarded after the first sight, unless utility, or some such variety as I have hinted at above continue to recommend it to their notice. And besides room for my Ware, I must have more room for my Ladys, for they sometimes come in very large shoals together, & one party are often obliged to wait till another have done their business.

Crucial to the fashionable success of Wedgwood's wares was his adoption of the antique style. He himself had limited acquaintance with the classics – but Bentley knew more, and he also had a good nose for what was popular. Excavations had begun at Pompeii in 1748. These were hardly scientific – twentieth-century archaeologists suggest that they did more damage than Vesuvius – but they had the effect of making Pompeii a five-star attraction on the Grand Tour.

By the late 1760s, architecture and interior design were showing a heavy classical influence, and Wedgwood extended this to pottery. Jasper Ware – the famous delicate stoneware with white figures in relief on a pastel-coloured

Wedgwood's early realization of the importance of the capital as a centre of fashion was a crucial factor in his success. His London showroom was laid out as carefully as an art exhibition, and provided a model for others to copy.

Wedgwood followed the fashion of the landed aristocracy by commissioning George Stubbs to paint this picture of his family in the grounds of Etruria Hall in 1780. (Right to left) Josiah Wedgwood, his wife Sarah and their children: John, Josiah II, Susannah, Catherine, Thomas, Sarah and Mary Anne. Stubbs spent several months at Etruria, giving drawing lessons to Wedgwood's sons, as well as producing his own work.

background – was intended from the start to harmonize with the interior decoration of such leading architects as Robert Adam.

The 'vase madness' of the 1770s saw Wedgwood developing a fine-grained Black Basalt that was also used for relief plaques, busts, medallions and cameos. He placed great faith in this new material, predicting that 'Black is Sterling and will last for ever.' Increasingly his pottery stretched into the realms of the ornamental and collectable, rather than the simply useful. Many pieces, such as a complete chess set in white Jasper, with blue-dipped or lilac stands, were developed in collaboration with artists such as John Flaxman.

Wedgwood had an eye for a good publicity stunt. The formal opening of his Etruria factory on 13 June 1769 had been marked by the production of six First Day's Vases, thrown by Wedgwood with the help of Bentley, who turned the wheel. (A youthful attack of smallpox had left his right knee so weakened that his leg had had to be amputated the previous year, and he was unable to use the kick wheel.)

More seriously, he had a shrewd understanding of marketing. His boldest move was the export drive which led him to send out large numbers of sample boxes on sale or return to the great noble households of Europe. They were generally accompanied by a personal note, written in flattering terms, such as that which he wrote to the Duke de Choiseul, Minister and Secretary of France:

Knowing the taste they have in France for every thing that comes from England, I thought your Excellency wou'd freely pardon the liberty I have taken to send you a box that contains a compleat apartment of Urns, & Vases in the antique taste, & after the Greek, Roman, & Etruscan models, & used for ornamenting apartments. This composition is the fruit of a manufacture lately established here under the immediate protection of the Queen, & for this reason called the Queen's Manufacture. The Apartment I take the liberty to address to your Excellency, is the same as one that hath been made here by order of the Empress of Russia, and hath been sent to the Kings of Denmark & Poland. The taste these different Princes have for these ornaments made me imagine they wou'd not displease your Excellency.

Wedgwood was taking liberties with the truth with his suggestion that his factory was under the same kind of direct royal patronage enjoyed by his European counterparts. He was also more than a little optimistic in his appraisal of the extent to which the French appreciated English style. Rococo was still dominant, bolstered by excise duties and edicts from Louis XV and Louis XVI to protect the Royal Manufactory from competition.

Not surprisingly, this particular approach failed – but, encouraged by other successes, Wedgwood decided to extend the sample package idea to the smaller states of Europe. This was a high-risk venture: his initial calculations suggested a cost of around £20,000 (more than £2 million-worth of pottery at today's prices). However, it was a risk that was clearly worth taking. By the 1780s, foreign sales accounted for an estimated 80 per cent of his production. By the 1790s, he had agents in Amsterdam, Antwerp, St Petersburg, Italy and many of the German states and principalities.

One recipient of a Wedgwood package was Prince Leopold Friedrich Franz of Anhalt-Dessau, an art patron and noted anglophile. His country estate in Wörlitz was in many ways a little England: he had even taken his gardeners with him to England, to learn about English landscape design. The result was effectively a complete exhibition centre of English style. From the very English garden, you could look through very English sash windows into some very English neo-classical rooms. It was an education in taste, and the perfect backdrop for Wedgwood's products.

Entry to the estate was free, and court members, aristocrats, academics and large numbers of the middle classes came to view this high-class showplace. Goethe, the great German writer and philosopher, made the first of several visits in 1776. He was charmed by the natural style of the gardens, but less sure about the taint of industry in the products in the house. In his view, industry killed art.

Included in the Prince's collection were over forty of the very fashionable black basalt 'Etruscan' vases. These were copies of ancient pottery pieces found by Sir William Hamilton in excavations in southern Italy. In fact, the originals on which they were based were Greek, rather than Etruscan,

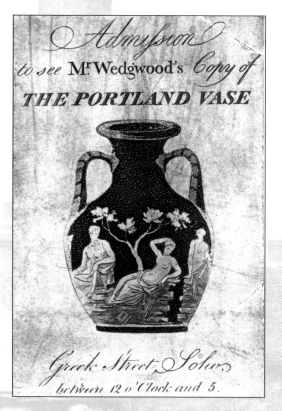

Admission to see Mr Wedgwood's Copy of THE PORTLAND VASE

Greek Street, Soho, between 12 o'Clock and 5.

Wedgwood made no secret of the fact that much of his work was copied from antique originals – in fact he used it as a marketing ploy. Ticket-only private views helped to confer exclusive status.

but Wedgwood was more interested in their marketing potential.

'There is a theory that Hamilton collected these vases, and he thought they were extremely valuable to the Greeks because they were found in their tombs,' explains Maxine Berg. 'But perhaps they weren't really so valuable to the Ancient Greeks. There is a very interesting theory that the vases were themselves copies of items made in gold and in silver. They were symbols of the wealth, the prestige of the person who died.

'Wedgwood made a copy of something that Hamilton had made appear very valuable, but perhaps wasn't. He really had made a brilliant move, making a copy of a copy and selling it as an extremely valuable, precious, rare item.'

The popularity of imitations of all kinds in the eighteenth century can be seen by a study of patents taken out during this period. From 1776 to 1800, for instance, a total of nineteen patents involving imitations were taken out. This figure included five for metal imitation buttons and shoe buckles, four for plating and tinning and three for ceramic imitation and ornamentation. Clearly Wedgwood was not the only one to discover the glories of imitation, but he set a pattern in the way that he used it to capture willing buyers across the whole social spectrum. The 'Vase Maker General' gave aristocrats copies of ancient vases they would have seen on the Grand Tour – and he gave the 'middling classes' affordable copies of vases from the great stately homes of England.

Always careful to protect his ideas with patents, Wedgwood was unusual for his time in his use of the personal trademark. 'Ornamental wares' were impressed with the Wedgwood and Bentley stamp; 'useful wares' with a plain Wedgwood. Meissen, in contrast, used a simple anonymous motif of crossed swords with a dot, changing to a star from 1780 onwards. This may not be particularly significant in itself, but the extent to which Wedgwood had the fashionable edge on Meissen in the eighteenth century is clearly illustrated by the case of Prince Franz. The Meissen manufactory was only 100 miles down the road – yet he chose to buy from England.

Part of the fashionable appeal of Wedgwood was the attraction of a style that used up-to-the-minute methods, but still looked back to the values of the great civilizations of Greece and Rome. Prince Franz was a reformer who admired the Enlightenment thinkers, and accordingly went for the English look.

'Wedgwood was the modern, the new,' says Maxine Berg. 'It seems that Meissen never picked up on this new fashion for earthenwares done in the neo-classical style. It had relied on a few designers who were stuck in the mould of the old designs that they'd made enormous successes on in the 1730s, but that was now passé. You might well ask: why didn't Prince Franz and others in Germany seek to set up their own factories to produce something that was even better than the Wedgwood style?

'In fact, during the Napoleonic blockades, when Prince Franz couldn't get what he wanted from the Wedgwood factories in England, he did promote and invest in a small factory in Dessau which would produce at least for his needs. But it didn't work. They couldn't produce the quality.

'Wedgwood had this whole network of workers in all kinds of skills, spread throughout Staffordshire, but also all over England. This was missing in Germany at the time, and so the factory failed after a few years, and Prince Franz died after that.'

The efficiency of Wedgwood's factory in Etruria lay not in automation, but in careful division of labour. It was the first pottery in Europe to be designed on the principle of the industrial assembly line, with long production runs of particular types of pottery. Materials were unloaded from the gates, or from the canal which ran at ground level in front of the factory. They progressed through the various workshops and kilns until they arrived back at the canal as finished goods for checking and despatch.

From the start, the factory was equipped with a water wheel, supplying power using water drawn from the canal. Wedgwood introduced the engine-turned lathe, which could be fitted with special tools to cut repetitive curved patterns, but mechanization was limited. The skill of the individual craftsman in the workshop was still all-important.

The factory at Etruria was designed to run alongside the canal, which Wedgwood had helped to promote in order to improve communications with London and Liverpool.

In the cotton industry, by contrast, increased mechanization had a vital part to play. This was matched by product marketing to create an up-market image for a fabric that had traditionally been thought of as utilitarian. Cotton clothes in a range of colours, imported from India, had been cheap enough for people to own several outfits. The trick was to persuade people that it could be fashionable, too – and for British manufacturers to start making it in profitable quantities themselves, to avoid having to import it. This import substitution, as economic historians term it, was what had provided the driving force behind the search for the secret of porcelain with which this chapter started.

At the end of the eighteenth century, Britain went mad for buying. There was one shop for every fifty people, an increasingly fashion-conscious pool of consumers, and an increasingly free market. (This last was one of several essential conditions for economic growth put forward by Adam Smith, Professor of Moral Philosophy at Glasgow University, in *An Inquiry into the Nature and Causes of the Wealth of Nations*, published in 1776.) The demand was there – and the cotton manufacturers jumped at the chance.

In 1765, half a million pounds of cotton had been spun in England, all of it by hand. By 1784, the figure had leapt to 12 million pounds, all spun by machine. The following year, the new Boulton and Watt steam engines were first used to power the spinning machinery at a factory in Papplewich, Nottinghamshire. This has been seen by many as the 'big bang' of the Industrial Revolution. Once the process of mechanization had also been applied to weaving, there was no going back. By 1812 the cost of cotton yarn was one-tenth of what it had been even in the 1770s and still falling. By 1830, finished cotton made up more than half of Britain's exports. All this from a country with not a cotton plantation in sight.

The advent of steam power meant that cotton mills no longer had to be sited next to running water. This in turn led directly to the growth of the great industrial cities which form part of most people's mental image of the Industrial Revolution. In 1830, one person in eighty in England worked in a cotton factory. However, it is important to keep a sense of proportion. Hand workers did not transform themselves into Hands as willingly or as easily as the foregoing account implies – Hands, with the capital 'H', used so pointedly by Charles Dickens in *Hard Times* to convey the dehumanizing effect of industrialization.

Mechanization in the cotton industry led to massive job losses. The first wave hit women spinners at home, who had no public platform, and no trade unions to support their cause. The second wave provided job opportunities for women and children in the factories – but many highly skilled, predominantly male weavers were left out in the cold. Some simply carried on weaving in dank cellars, for lower and lower wages. Some, more articulate, voiced their despair through trade unions and through newspapers. A Royal Commission on hand-loom weaving was set up, but the change was irreversible. Other parts of the textile industry were slower to become automated. A group of women weavers in Yorkshire, for instance, managed to maintain their independence by setting up a co-operative woollen mill. They carried on weaving at home, only bringing their cloth into the mill to be finished. In Coventry, some silk weavers invented a half-way house to the factory system. Their cottages were lined up along a court, with a steam engine at one end, and an engine shaft running through the houses. Workers paid rent to hook up to the power source, and this helped them to maintain a semi-independent status for a while. In the end, though, both these examples were simply rearguard actions in the face of the inevitable.

Luddite outbreaks, strikes and food riots – prompted by high prices and poor harvests – were clear symptoms of working-class discontent in Britain. However, the question has to be asked: why was there not more protest against the new machinery? On the Continent, by contrast, the guilds had managed to resist the introduction of automation. In France, ironically, this was because everything was controlled by the State. If you managed to stop the agent of the State in the person of a Vaucanson, you effectively stopped the whole mechanization parade. In Britain, new factories were started not by the government, but by small-scale entrepreneurs. They were set up far from traditional craft centres, and far from the influence of guilds. Energetic resistance might thwart one such enterprise, but there would always be others.

Odd though it might seem, the heyday of the Industrial Revolution in Britain coincided with a period of war. The French and Napoleonic wars led to a huge national debt, and the imposition for the first time of income tax. The French Revolution had shown what could happen when a country got its taxation system wrong. In Britain, the government managed to raise enough money without triggering rebellion, although this was a pretty close-run thing at times. Some historians have suggested that the years between the Battle of Waterloo in 1815 and the Massacre of Peterloo in 1819 were the nearest Britain has ever come to social revolution. Given its name as an ironic analogy to the famous battle, Peterloo was an initially peaceful political reform meeting, held in St Peter's Fields outside Manchester. It ended in disaster when a cavalry charge left eleven workers dead and over 400 wounded.

Domestic troubles apart, the wars fought during the period covered by this chapter had the great advantage for Britain of being fought on foreign soil. This kept the arms-makers busy without the whole country being turned into a battlefield. Taxation enabled the government to ride out economic blockades, but was not sufficiently crushing to prevent people from spending money on the new consumer goods. When Napoleon dismissed Britain as being a nation of shopkeepers, he may have been pointing to a factor in his own defeat.

By 1830, fifteen years after the final victory over Napoleon, when the *Rocket* made its journey from Liverpool to Manchester, consumer capitalism was well developed in Britain. Travellers, industrial spies and the merely curious came to see a spectacle they found both awesome and frightening.

'Manchester became a kind of dark tourist attraction during the 1820s and 1830s,' says Simon Schaffer. 'Lots of people really did come to look at what was going on, and they thought it was a mixture of hell and the future. The game was going to be how to tease out which bits of what was going on you actually wanted to salvage, and which you didn't want, which was most of it. You didn't want the vast sprawl of the industrial city, the huge clouds of smoke and a world gone mad, as most observers thought.'

Foreigners were not the only people to feel the need to investigate this new industrial nation. William Cobbett left his southern base at the beginning of 1830 for a northern tour, and much of his description reads like that of a tourist in a foreign country.

All the way along from Leeds to Sheffield it is coal and iron, and iron and coal. It was dark before we reached Sheffield; so that we saw the iron furnaces in all the horrible splendour of their everlasting blaze. Nothing can be

The Massacre of Peterloo, in which an unarmed crowd was hacked down by mounted cavalry. More than 60,000 men, women and children had gathered to hear a speech by a radical farmer, Henry Hunt. The reference to a 'vote of thanks' is a reminder of one of their grievances: the fact that Manchester, England's second largest city, had no member of parliament.

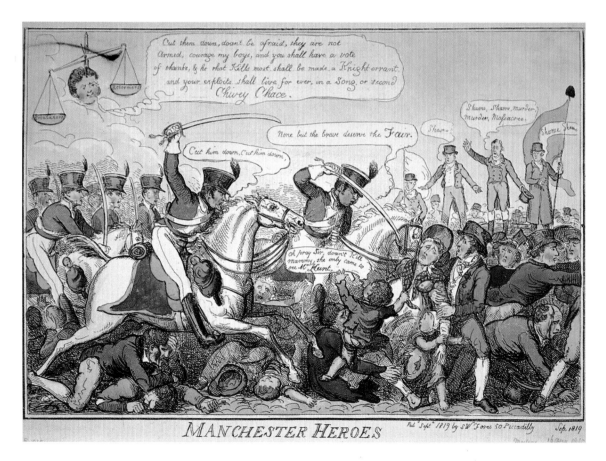

Loyal Address & Radical Petitions, or the R——ts most gracious answer to both sides of the question at once

George Cruickshank's *Loyal Addresses and Radical Petitions, 1819* gives another bitterly sarcastic view on the Establishment's reaction to Peterloo. The Prince Regent — the future King George IV — is seen giving a gracious reception to a group of loyal sycophants, while emitting a blast of noxious gases in the faces of radical reformers.

conceived more grand or more terrific than the yellow waves of fire that incessantly issue from the top of these furnaces. … It is a surprising thing to behold; and it is impossible to behold it without being convinced that, whatever other nations may do with cotton and with wool, they will never equal England with regard to things made of iron and steel. This Sheffield, and the land all about it, is one bed of iron and coal. They call it black Sheffield, and black enough it is; but from this one town and its environs go nine-tenths of the knives that are used in the whole world; there being, I understand, no knives made at Birmingham; the manufacture of which place consists of the larger sort of implements, of locks of all sorts, and guns and swords, and of all the endless articles of hardware which go to the furnishing of a house.

Iron and coal … blackness … all are irreversibly entangled in the picture of Britain at this point, according to Alan Macfarlane.

'Our civilization in the modern world is built first on coal and later of course on other carbon energy – oil, and so on,' he says. 'Without this, there could have been no Industrial Revolution, it couldn't have happened in England and we would still be living in an agrarian society.

'It affected all power and production, but it may have also changed our visual world. It's been suggested that possibly having black buildings around you, having smoke going out of the chimneys, having coal, having black iron, meant that everything became black. You think about the

LEFT: Mourners follow a plume-draped hearse in a typical Victorian funeral — a reminder of the all-pervasive influence of the colour black in the nineteenth century.

Victorian period and you think of the black hats, the black funerals, the Black Country. Blackness, coal, industry, iron – all come together.

'We live in an age which has moved away from that blackness, but we went through it, and without that we would not have reached where we are. It is an extraordinary transformation, based on this particular substance.'

A glance at events in the century leading up to 1830 has shown some reasons why Britain had the edge on its near neighbours in this transformation. The Germans could not imagine a market beyond their nobility. The French may have had their gifted inventors, but they could not strike the right balance between man and the machine. They were also diverted by the small matter of a revolution. Britain had relative stability, a tolerant, clubbish society that encouraged individualism, and an expanding population that created a market for new mass-produced products. Perhaps the X factor with which we started this chapter was a unique combination of all these things.

However, none of this really explains why western Europe had the edge on the rest of the world. For a fuller explanation of the puzzle, we need to cross the Atlantic and Pacific oceans, to follow the great merchant ships and expand the time frame to 250 years.

OPPOSITE: *Iron and Coal* by William Bell Scott, a mural from Wallington Hall, Northumberland, shows the dark energy of the Industrial Revolution. Ironworkers wield hammers, while behind them stands a pit boy with his Davy lamp. In the background, a train steams across Robert Stephenson's high-level bridge. Even the little girl in front subscribes to the work ethic: on her lap is a book of arithmetic.

Chapter Three

SHIPS OF FORTUNE

250 YEARS

Time: 1600–1850
Place: Western Europe—
North America—
The Ottoman
Empire

So far, we have trodden some fairly familiar territory in our discussion of the massive explosion of energy that was the Industrial Revolution. Clearly, there were many things that were special about Britain in the eighteenth and nineteenth centuries. However, this is still a less than full explanation of why the culture of our particular damp corner of Europe colonized the world.

If we look back to 1600, Britain was only a small power on the edge of a war-torn civilization. The Netherlands, with colonies in five continents, was far from the little backwater that the poet Andrew Marvell liked to think when he wrote so disparagingly in 'The Character of Holland':

Holland, that scarce deserves the name of land,
As but the off-scouring of the British sand.

Nor was there cause for self-satisfaction about Britain's chances of economic or military development compared to that of the Ottoman Empire, which throughout the previous century had appeared to be sweeping all before it. Many Christians feared the spread of Islam in much the same way that, in the twentieth century, at the height of the Cold War, Westerners feared Communism.

Both The Netherlands and the Ottoman Empire were dominant, confident and cultured nations which appeared to have many of the ingredients of a modern industrial society. Yet by 1850, both had been overtaken by Britain. The puzzle our group of historians aimed to explore is: why?

Much of the action of this chapter takes place at sea, with the British navy – which in 1588 had just narrowly escaped a drubbing from the Spanish Armada – and with the great ships of exploration. This was a period of intense curiosity about the world, and the opening up of new trade routes went hand in hand with the search for exotic objects and useful plants. Conquering and understanding nature was a goal shared by scientists and merchants alike, and the symbiotic relationship between science and commerce is an important part of our story.

In September 1609, a sailing ship called the *Half Moon* nosed its way up a river, past an island that was later to be called Manhattan. The captain was an Englishman, Henry Hudson, and his mission was to find a new route to China. Nobody, either on or off the ship, would have made the slightest guess that the island they were passing (where, the captain recorded, the natives were particularly hostile and rude) would one day be the greatest city of its age. Manhattan was just a means to an end.

The holy grail of northern Europeans at this time was the search for a shorter route to the East, avoiding the stormy and time-consuming haul around the Cape of Good Hope and Cape Horn. Hudson had attempted to go directly over the North Pole, and he had tried a north-eastern route above Siberia. Both times, he had been turned back by pack ice. Now, he was looking for a passage to the North West. No one had any idea how broad the American continent was, so, as far as he was concerned, what we know as the Hudson River could have led to the Pacific at any minute. In fact, it led him to Albany.

Joel Mokyr, sees this search for the most economical ways to trade as one of the things that set Europeans apart at this time. The other was the way explorers shopped around in the search for financial backing. Hudson was an Englishman, yet he was sailing on a Dutch ship, with a Dutch crew, paid for by the Dutch East India Company.

'Loyalty to your country was definitely secondary to the need to carry out these voyages,' says Professor Mokyr. 'In some sense this underlies one of the secrets of Europe – the competition of the State system within Europe meant that nobody could afford to fall very much behind. If you did, and

A typical flat and windswept Dutch landscape in *The Shore at Egmond-aan-Zee* by Jacob van Ruisdael.

Hudson's Last Voyage by J. Collier depicts the icy fate that awaited the great explorer. Hudson is pictured with his teenage son, John.

it sometimes happened, you just disappeared off the political map. This is what happened to both Spain and Portugal at some point in the middle of the seventeenth century. They stopped playing the game, and so the Dutch and the French and the English took it over.

'If it had happened that some very powerful ruler had managed to effectively unite Europe under one government and then the son of the ruler had said: "I really don't want anybody to make waves, I like things the way they are, let's honour our traditions", perhaps innovativeness in Europe would have stopped and we would have never had an industrial revolution.'

The downside to all this inter-State competition, of course, was the huge waste of human life and hardware caused by the apparently constant European wars that dominated this period of history. The British fought both the French and the Dutch at different times and, even when no shots were being fired, trade rivalry was intense. This was amply illustrated by Henry Hudson's fate when he returned to London. His ship was seized, the ship's log with all its valuable information impounded, and the crew thrown into jail. He himself was forbidden ever again to sail with anything but a British crew. In 1610, obedient to orders, he set out on a British-financed mission, reaching what is now called Hudson Bay. The crew mutinied, he was set adrift in a small boat with his son and seven other seamen, and they were never seen again.

The heavy-handed British attempt to keep the Dutch out of North America did not work in the short term. Dutch fur traders followed Henry Hudson's route, and established a toehold in what is now the financial district of New York. In 1626, the Dutch bought Manhattan from the Indians, and the first boatload of settlers landed at the place they called New Amsterdam. By the mid seventeenth century, this was a thriving town of a thousand inhabitants, protected to the south by a fort and to the north by a wooden wall (the origin of the name Wall Street). The houses had characteristic Dutch gables and tile roofs – and, to make the occupants feel at home, there was even a windmill and a canal.

Canals, of course, are inextricably associated in most people's minds with the original Amsterdam. To the modern tourist, they are part of its antique charm – but in the early part of the seventeenth century, they were essential arteries in what was then the richest city in the world. This was the golden age of The Netherlands, which had fleets controlling crucial sea lanes, and merchants regulating world markets. Sea travel and trade were so important to the Dutch that they planned Amsterdam as a system of concentric canals, bringing the sea into the heart of their city. Anyone with a bit of extra attic space and a hoisting beam could make a fast florin or two – and many made small fortunes through trading on the canal.

Amsterdam was an international market for goods from all over the world: Japanese and Swedish copper, Baltic grain, oriental tea, Indonesian spices, Mexican silver. As Daniel Defoe put it: 'They are the factors and brokers of Europe. They buy to sell again, take in to send out, and the greatest part of their vast commerce consists in being supply'd from all parts of the world, that they may supply all the world again.'

As a new city, Amsterdam was especially receptive to changing patterns of trade, and its expansion was rapid. In 1600, two years before the founding of the Dutch East India Company, it had a population of 50,000. By 1662, this had quadrupled to 200,000. Its people were thrifty and hard-working, and there was a ready pool of brave and hardy sailors to man some of the best ships in the world.

The Return to Amsterdam of the Fleet of the Dutch East India Company by Andries van Eertvelt. The company, which used powerful warships, had a monopoly over Dutch trade and navigation.

The rewards of successful seagoing expeditions were enormous. From its earliest days of trading, the Dutch East India Company planned each venture meticulously. Captains would even be told exactly which part of their ship they should use to store particular types of cargo. Spices were particularly good value, as they took up so little space, but they were easily spoiled. The ships sailed with a minimum of crew, and each vessel could easily pay for itself on a single trip – but only, of course, if it returned safely. Shipping insurance was a growth industry.

Conditions on board were grim. Sailors slept on old sails or coils of line on the hard wood decks. If one crew member came down with a disease such as dysentery, it would immediately spread throughout the ship. Malnutrition was rife, as food was maggoty and infested with worms, and fresh fruit and vegetables were scarce. The fire risk of cooking in a storm meant that they could have hot food only in calm weather (when, presumably, they least needed it). If the ship was damaged at sea, the crew had to be able to repair it on the spot if they wanted to survive.

When the *Half Moon* lost its foremast on its original voyage, the ship's carpenter was simply sent ashore for a new one. He returned three days later, they hauled the new foremast aboard the ship in the morning, and it was fully rigged by the afternoon. This was no mean task, considering the network of ropes and sails it supported – but the ship's log appeared to be more interested in their fishing tally: thirty-eight lobsters and forty-five cod fish.

Early explorers like Columbus had had royal patronage, and a religious mission. Henry Hudson and others like him were sponsored by private companies, and they realized that commercial spin-offs were vital if they wanted money for future voyages. Even if they did not achieve the prime purpose of their trip, they could still come back with a full hold. In the case of the Dutch, their holds were fuller than most, as their ships were so deep. This meant that when they had to pay taxes in foreign ports, they were undercharged by some 10 to 15 per cent, as the usual rule of thumb for calculating taxes was based on smaller ships.

The Dutch, like other Europeans, faced the problem of having very little to offer in exchange for the goods that they wanted from foreign ports. However, they developed some canny sidelines on established trade routes which ensured that their ships rarely sailed empty. In North America, for example, they acted as middlemen in the exchange of wampum, the beads made from shells that the American Indians used as currency. Those who lived in the woodlands had stacks of the beaver pelts that the Dutch wanted, but very little wampum. The Dutch, with the help of Indians living on the coast, were happy to oblige.

Predominantly a Protestant nation, The Netherlands in the seventeenth century was an open, tolerant society that had become a haven for Jews and other persecuted minorities. People were free to develop their businesses irrespective of race or religion, and an atmosphere of healthy competition was fostered. A key factor in industrialization is, of course, a ready source of capital – and in this, too, the Dutch scored. They had financial institutions that were to become the envy of the world, and a serious-minded attitude towards investment.

Investment, however, could go wrong, as some ordinary citizens found to their cost. Take the tulip, for example, that most Dutch of all flowers. Enterprising merchants could see that this popular bulb might be a good way of making easy money, and soon bulbs were changing hands for truly silly prices. Particularly rare tulips were given the names of Dutch admirals: the 'Admiral Liefkin' was worth 4,400 florins – a tidy sum at a time when the average annual income was about 150 florins. The highest recorded price for a single bulb was 13,000 florins – more than the cost of the most expensive canal-side house in the centre of Amsterdam.

The extent to which these nondescript-looking bulbs were valued is illustrated by the story of the sailor who decided to spice up his breakfast with what he thought was an onion he had found lying around. Unfortunately for him, the 'onion' was a 3,000-florin 'Semper Augustus' tulip bulb. The sailor – having eaten the evidence – was later charged with stealing the tulip, and was thrown into gaol.

People from all classes joined in the tulip madness, naïvely assuming that the bulbs would hold their value for ever. Some used their life savings, others used money that should have been spent on food or rent. Credit was also readily available from the Bank of Amsterdam, which had been founded in 1609. When the investment bubble burst in 1636, many ordinary people were ruined. The episode showed all too clearly just how fragile confidence could be in this new type of speculative society. Sadly, as we will see, the tulip fanciers were by no means the last group in history to fall victim to such illusory dreams of wealth.

At the height of the tulip madness, rich merchants had kept their treasured bulbs locked away and under tight security, commissioning paintings of the flowers in bloom to remind them of their investment. Once the bulbs lost their value, the pictures then became treasured in their own right. Amsterdam was

Striped tulips were the most highly prized by collectors. The stripes were actually the result of a virus, but they gave the bulbs rarity value.

an international marketplace for art as for everything else, and the great paintings of the Dutch golden age are among its most memorable relics. Rembrandt, Frans Hals and Vermeer may be the names most popularly associated with this period, but there were many, many others.

Traditionally, the Church had been an important patron of art, but imagery in Church buildings was not acceptable to the austere Calvinists, who were the source of many artistic commissions. Artists increasingly turned away from religious subjects to portraits and studies of everyday life, their paintings becoming smaller and more intimate. The merchants and civic leaders who had made Amsterdam the richest city in the world had a strong urge for immortality on canvas, and they paid well. Across the centuries, their images stare out at us with unblinking confidence.

However, they did not remain masters of the universe for ever, and the puzzle is: why not? Joel Mokyr thinks the answer is partly because they had their industrial revolution too early.

'It often gets overlooked how much of the Dutch success story is actually based on technological advances,' he says. 'This wasn't just a society that was very good at buying and selling. A large number of new products and techniques emanated from Holland during this golden age.'

Among the ideas that could have led Holland to greatness were two vital scientific instruments, both invented by Dutch opticians: the compound microscope, by Zacharias Jansen in 1590, and the telescope, by Johann Lippersheim in 1605. There were numerous other brilliant and

These serious-minded officers of the Amsterdam Coopers' and Wine-rackers' Guild are depicted with the ledgers and seals that symbolize their success. In the background is a picture of their patron saint, St Matthias.

practical Dutch gadgets. However, these inventions were still extensions of medieval and Renaissance technology, according to Joel Mokyr. The honours were to go to the country that could come up with original inventions, *and* produce them on a mass scale. As he puts it: 'There was no question that by, say, 1615, The Netherlands was where the action was. It was after 1650 that they had to share it with other countries as well.'

An increasingly conservative guild system resisted innovation, and the relatively small size of the country with its limited natural resources also hindered growth. The Dutch were very good at making the most of what they had. The flatness of their countryside, for instance, meant that there was no fast-flowing water to provide power – but it proved ideal territory for windmills. Similarly, they had no coal – so they used peat instead. In the end, though, this was another limiting factor, as peat cannot compete with coal for intensity of heat.

In Britain, coal had been an essential element in the growth of industry. Medieval people had been prejudiced against this smelly source of fuel, preferring instead to chop down the great forests. However, as wood supplies started to dwindle, they were forced to start digging for coal. This black gold was used not only to heat houses, but to bake bricks, refine sugar, brew beer, make glass and smelt iron.

The coal revolution in turn produced the canal revolution, since the only way to transport such a heavy commodity before the advent of serviceable roads and railways was by water. By the 1600s, boats were carrying coal along

A Windmill by a River by Jan van Goyen is a reminder of how the Dutch used the natural flatness of their landscape to their own advantage.

the coast from Newcastle to London, and along the river from Coalbrookdale to Bristol. In 1694, work started on making the Mersey navigable as far as Warrington and, by the mid eighteenth century, dredging and improving of rivers had turned into the construction of a network of canals. The connection between coal and the new canals was made explicit by the Duke of Bridgewater's comment: 'A good canal should have coal at the heels of it.'

Meanwhile, on the high seas, the British had decided to end Dutch domination. Their own East India Company had made its first voyage with a fleet of five ships in 1601. Like its Dutch equivalent, it had spices in its sights – but, initially, the oceans seemed wide enough for everyone. An East India Company captain in 1603 recorded a stop at St Helena where they relieved the starving crews of French and Dutch vessels with six hogsheads of pork, two of fish, one of beans, and 500 of bread. As they were taking home 1,030,000 pounds of pepper, they probably felt they could afford to be generous.

In fact it was friction over pepper, an essential commodity increasingly monopolized by the Dutch, that at one point threatened to erupt into outright war in the spice islands. Nearer home, the fierce hold of the sturdy Dutch boats carrying on trade in the North Sea, Baltic and English Channel was making the English jealous. Deciding to take drastic action, they passed

King Charles II rides in a triumphal procession to Whitehall (1660), site of his father's execution eleven years earlier. Despite such dramatic political events at home, it was business as usual on the high seas.

a series of Navigation Acts which effectively banned Dutch boats from bringing foreign goods into British ports, and then backed this up with military force.

The First Navigation Act was passed in 1651, two years after the execution of Charles I. It was followed by another in 1660 – a date more usually associated in people's minds with the restoration of Charles II. These were troubled times at home, as indicated by the tone of relief in the diary entry of the royalist, John Evelyn, for 29 May 1660:

This day, his Majesty, Charles the Second came to London, after a sad and long exile and calamitous suffering both of the King and Church, being seventeen years. This was also his birthday, and with a triumph of above 20,000 horse and foot, brandishing their swords, and shouting with inexpressible joy; the ways strewed with flowers, the bells ringing, the streets hung with tapestry, fountains running with wine; the Mayor, Aldermen, and all the Companies, in their liveries, chains of gold, and banners; Lords and Nobles, clad in cloth of silver, gold, and velvet; the windows and balconies, all set with ladies; trumpets, music, and myriads of people flocking, even so far as from Rochester, so as they were seven hours in passing the city, even from two in the afternoon till nine at night.

It does suggest a degree of singlemindedness that a country could pay so much attention to its overseas trade while embroiled in a bloody civil war and the inevitable patching-up process that followed it.

Across the Atlantic, Britain was finding the presence of the Dutch settlement in New Amsterdam increasingly irritating, given that the flag of St George now fluttered along the rest of the coast. Charles II granted the area to his brother, the Duke of York (later James II); it was captured in 1664 and renamed New York. However, the city never forgot its Dutch roots. New Amsterdam had been exceptionally tolerant and egalitarian. Women could inherit estates from their husbands, and inter-racial marriages were acceptable. Both were unusual at the time, and some see this openness as a vital part of the capitalist success story that New York was to become.

British ships had been unofficially at war with the Dutch wherever they shared the same waters, and in 1665 war became official. Both sides claimed victory in sea battles, but things took an ugly turn after a British raiding party pillaged the prosperous town of Terschelling, on 9 August 1666. The Dutch saw the Great Fire of London, which broke out three weeks later, as God's retribution for this attack. However, not content with this, they launched a daring raid up the River Medway the following year.

In the aftermath of the plague and the Great Fire, Britain had been left so strapped for cash that the astonishing decision had been taken to lay up the fleet for the winter, and not prepare a new one. Admittedly, peace negotiations with Holland had been opened, but relying on sea defences to protect the fleet in harbour was to prove foolhardy in the extreme. The Dutch sailed up the Medway in June 1667. Within four days, they had burnt or sunk almost every boat they could find, halting in their progress only after the British, in desperation, scuttled ships in their path.

Faced with such a trouncing, it is understandable that contemporaries made the most of stories such as the bravery of Captain Archibald Douglas, who alone of all his men stayed at his post on the *Royal Oak* to the last. In his poem 'The Loyal Scot', Andrew Marvell wrote:

Fixed on his ship he faced the horrid day,
And wondered much at those who run away:
Nor other fear himself could comprehend
Then, least heaven fall ere thither he ascend,
But entertains the while his time too short
With birding at the Dutch, as if in sport …

Like a glad lover the fierce flames he meets,
And tries his first embraces in their sheets.
His shape exact, which the bright flames enfold,
Like the sun's statue stands of burnished gold.

The reality which lay behind such stories is evident in the diary of Samuel Pepys, uniquely placed to form a true assessment of morale in his role as Surveyor General of the Victualling Office for the Navy. He wrote, sadly: 'the hearts as well as affections of the seamen are turned away; and in the open streets in Wapping, and up and down, the wives have cried publicly, "This comes of your not paying our husbands …". Most people that I speak with are in doubt how we shall do to secure our seamen from running over to the Dutch; which is a sad but very true consideration at this day.'

After hearing of the success of the Dutch in breaking the defensive chain at Chatham, he wrote: 'to White Hall to hear the truth of it; and there going up the Park-stairs I did hear some lacquies speaking of sad news come to Court, saying, there is hardly anybody in the Court but do look as if he cried … the truth is I do fear so much that the whole Kingdom is undone, that I do this night resolve to study with my father and wife what to do with the little that I have in money by me.'

On 13 June he recorded that he had made his will, giving everything he had equally between his father and his wife. Similarly, his friend and fellow diarist John Evelyn noted that he had sent his best plate for safe-keeping away from the house, prompted by fears that the Dutch would sail up the Thames to London. On Monday 17 June he described how a fire on an English ship at Deptford Yard caused mass panic after it was rumoured that the Dutch were landing.

The Treaty of Breda in July 1667 ended the war, but the whole sorry episode is a salient reminder of the dangers of smug satisfaction offered by a wider historical perspective. It is all too easy to gloss over events that do not fit into a Voltairean picture of everything being for the best, in the best of all possible worlds.

In fact, only two decades later, the Dutch *did* invade Britain – quite peacefully, and by invitation. Dissatisfaction with the arrogant Catholic King James II led to the bloodless Glorious Revolution, and the arrival in England of William III and Mary II in 1688. Many people had been worried that James was set to turn Britain into a Catholic country – worries that were brought into focus by the birth of a son, offering the prospect of a Catholic succession. James's daughter, Mary – a staunch Anglican – was married to William of Orange, so the pair were an obvious choice for the increasingly restless British aristocracy. They invited them to Britain; James made a half-hearted attempt to fight, dithered, then fled ignominiously to exile in France.

As a high-ranking officer in the Admiralty, Samuel Pepys saw morale in the navy reach an all-time low. His true fears were expressed in his diary, written in code.

So, having failed to defeat the Dutch, the English increasingly started to copy them. This had been the case for some time at sea. Now, Dutch influence extended into every sphere – most notably, for our purposes, that of commerce and finance. With a new political settlement offering relative stability, the English economy was open for business.

Crucial to this process was the establishment of the Bank of England in 1694. Banking on a small scale was already well established, but this was to be the bank to end all banks. The idea had first been put forward by a London-based Scots entrepreneur, William Paterson. His original proposal was rejected partly because, as he wrote in 1695: '[people] said this project came from Holland and therefore would not hear of it, since we had too many Dutch things already'. Eventually, with the support of the Chancellor of the Exchequer and a leading merchant in the City, the scheme was approved by Parliament.

The plan was to encourage the public to invest, thus providing ready money for the government to borrow whenever necessary. William was particularly keen on this, as he wanted to support his native country in its war against the French. The Bank's first home was Mercers' Hall in Cheapside. It started with £1,200,000, deposited by those happy to help the war if it meant gaining an 8 per cent return on their capital. In exchange for lending money to the government, the Bank was granted a Royal Charter, and it became the heart of what we now know as the City. New financial institutions of all kinds sprang up, together with a new breed of professionals who dealt with 'imaginary money', or investments on paper.

The idea that property was not necessarily something you could put your hand on gained increasing currency. Of course, as the Dutch had discovered with the tulips crash, speculating was a risky business. The best-known example in England in the early eighteenth century was the South Sea Company, which competed with the Bank of England in aiming to take over the National Debt. The company claimed it would send ships to trade in the South Seas; in fact, this was only so much hot air. People invested their life savings in shares whose value rose by 1,000 per cent – and, when there was a sudden crisis of confidence, they were left with valueless scraps of paper.

For the most part, though, the eighteenth century saw a growth of confidence in new ways of dealing. Shares, bills of exchange, and the first banknotes all became a normal part of the credit economy – and these in their turn helped new businesses to flourish. Towards the end of the century, as the Dutch became increasingly sidetracked by two decades of war against the French, the English economy started to take off in a big way. With a larger population, and greater natural resources, they were set to overtake their one-time rivals. They had learnt the lessons of success from the Dutch, and beaten them at their own game.

Meanwhile, where was the rest of the world in all this? Back in 1609, while Henry Hudson had been sailing up the river in North America, the first stones of the mosque of Sultan Ahmed were being laid in Istanbul. Known to the world as the Blue Mosque, this magnificent building at the heart of the Ottoman Empire symbolized its confidence and pride. Throughout the previous century, they had seemed unbeatable – and, indeed, it was their domination of the trade routes to the East that had led Henry Hudson and others like him to look for a short cut to avoid them.

Islamic world takeover was a major fear at the beginning of the seventeenth century. A good illustration of this is a history of English voyages called *Purchas his Pilgrimes, contayning a History of the World in Sea Voyages and Land Travell by Englishmen and others*, published in 1625. The author of this monumental work was a vicar called Samuel Purchas, who – according to Simon Schaffer – was very keen to convince his countrymen that all major successful explorations had been made by Englishmen.

The Royal Exchange and the Bank of England, 1851. The neo-classical architecture expressed confidence in new ways of financial dealing. As the government needed more money, the Bank of England expanded into grander premises.

'The first map which Purchas put into his book was a map of the world with Hudson's voyages and so on all marked,' says Simon Schaffer. 'But the most important thing on the map was that it showed you symbolically which parts of the world were Christian and which parts were Muslim. All the Christian bits were carefully marked with crosses, and all the Muslim bits carefully marked with crescents.

'Purchas was very, very worried because he knew from Dutch voyages that Islam was expanding into what is now the East Indies and Indonesia, and that Islam was very powerful indeed in West Africa, which was one of the main European sources of gold. It looked to Purchas as if Islam was about to take over the whole planet, and only Protestant England and The Netherlands could save Christendom and therefore, as he understood it, civilization from total eclipse.'

However, according to Joel Mokyr, contemporaries had less to fear than they supposed. 'There were interesting hints even at that time that if they had looked closer should have perhaps reassured them a little bit,' he says. 'One of them was how much Europeans actually knew about Islam. They were studying the language, they were studying the institutions, they were looking around seeing what these people knew that we didn't know that we could possibly copy.

'What is interesting is that on most issues that matter, Islamic civilization didn't return the favour. They did not study Christianity, they did not try to learn their languages, the only item of the Christian world's technologies that they were willing to adopt – and even that they did quite willy-nilly – was firearms. It might also be pointed out that they were very slow in adopting the printing press. The first book printed in Arabic that is known of was printed in 1717, more than two and a half centuries after the Gutenberg press.'

A shortage of iron and skilled iron workers was one practical reason why metal printing took so long to reach the Ottoman Empire. Also, the scribes who produced elaborate calligraphic versions of the Koran had a vested interest in spreading fears that any replacement technology might distort the word of God by printing mistakes. Joel Mokyr quotes a saying attributed to the Prophet Muhammad that 'whoever imitates a people becomes one of them' as an explanation for a general reluctance to copy Western technology. Openness to new ideas is a crucial factor in industrialization. In the Ottoman Empire, however, religion and political conservatism, together with resistance to innovation, conspired against this.

The golden age of the Ottoman Empire had been synonymous with the name of the ruler known in the West as Suleyman the Magnificent. Ruling from 1520 to 1566, he reformed administration, encouraged vast architectural and cultural projects, and proved himself an expert military strategist. During his reign, the tentacles of Islam stretched to include Belgrade,

Under Suleyman the Magnificent, the Ottoman Empire reached its point of greatest expansion over Asia and Europe.

Budapest, Rhodes, Tabriz, Baghdad, Aden and Algiers. Even though he did not occupy Roman lands, he still claimed them as his own. In inscriptions, he called himself: 'Slave of God, powerful with the power of God, deputy of God on earth, obeying the commands of the *Qur'an* and enforcing them throughout the world, master of all lands, the shadow of God over all nations, Sultan of Sultans in all the lands of Persians and Arabs, the propagator of Sultanic laws.'

The name Suleyman translates into English as Solomon, and this most respected of all rulers was known in his own country as Suleyman the Lawgiver. In Islamic political theory, the central function of the sultan was to guarantee justice – and the model of the just ruler was Solomon in the Hebrew histories. Suleyman the Magnificent was seen as a second Solomon.

Sultans wielded enormous personal power, which clearly had severe disadvantages with less Solomon-like rulers, such as Suleyman's successor, known in Islamic history as Selim the Drunkard. In the absence of clear central authority, power went by default to the military, and an increasingly corrupt bureaucracy.

Part of the problem lay in the rules of succession, which were dominated by the fear of rebellion. Traditionally, once a sultan had assumed the throne, all his brothers as well as their sons would have been killed. This practice was stopped by the late sixteenth century, but the fear of conflict caused by rival claims to the throne remained. Instead of killing the spare males, the sultans took to locking them away in the harem. They lived in splendid isolation, eating and drinking their lives away. In the case of Suleyman the Magnificent, the son he had groomed to succeed him as sultan betrayed him. He was forced to have him executed, and to reclaim the lazy and incompetent Selim from the harem. Untrained in military or government affairs, it is perhaps not so surprising that Selim was not very interested.

Considering the vast area that came under its control, the Ottoman Empire at its height had a relatively low population: an estimated 28,000,000 people in 1600. Plague remained endemic as late as the early nineteenth century, long after it had been virtually eliminated elsewhere. Historians argue about the causes of this, but a tendency to regard disease as the will of God, and a failure to take quarantine measures similar to those in place in Europe cannot have helped matters. Forty thousand people died in an epidemic of plague in Constantinople in 1770. Between 1812 and 1814, the disease claimed a third of the populations of Bucharest and Belgrade. Many rural areas became depopulated, resulting in inevitable periods of famine.

It is, of course, important not to generalize. The Ottomans may not have been able to halt the plague, but in at least one respect their medicine was a step ahead of the Western world. Inoculation against smallpox was an established part of Turkish folk medicine. Lady Mary Wortley Montagu, wife of the British Ambassador to Turkey, had been badly marked by the disease herself. Keen that others should not suffer in the same way, she introduced the technique into England. In a letter home on April 1716, she gave a graphic description of the process, which involved inducing a mild attack of the disease which left the patient ill for two or three days, but rarely scarred. She wrote: 'Every year thousands undergo this operation; and the French ambassador says pleasantly, that they take the small-pox here by way of diversion, as they take the waters in other countries. There is no example of anyone that has died in it; and you may believe I am well satisfied of the safety of this experiment, since I intend to try it on my dear little son.'

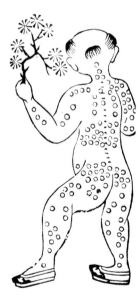

An eighteenth-century engraving of a child with smallpox. The idea of vaccination came to Turkey from China, where it had been known since the tenth century.

Although this technique – inoculation with weakened smallpox virus – was to be superseded by Jenner's development of vaccination with the cowpox virus, it was undoubtedly a very advanced method for its time.

Ottoman craftsmen had been worldbeaters, and magnificently carved scientific instruments such as astrolabes were the envy of the West. Such devices were a crystallized, solid form of theoretical knowledge. An astrolabe enabled the observer to track the movements of the suns and stars, and understand astronomy in a very practical way. However, the balance between science, religion and the State became increasingly uneasy. In 1580, the Ottoman army razed an observatory to the ground, on the pretext that astronomical observations caused the plague.

However, in the application of science to manufacturing, industrialization remained a distant prospect. The problems of the Ottoman Empire in mass-producing and stockpiling goods to meet demand have been compared to those faced by the Communist Soviet Union in the mid twentieth century. It is an interesting parallel on the domestic front – but, unlike Soviet Russia, the Ottoman Empire's cultural isolation also extended to military technology.

Many engravings were made to commemorate victory over the Turks at the Siege of Vienna on 12 September 1683. The static heavy guns on which the Turks relied can be seen in the foreground.

This was seen most clearly as the Empire found itself out-gunned in war, despite centuries of meticulously copying captured firearms. The Turks had won the Siege of Constantinople in 1453 with heavy siege guns – but they failed to realize that the world had moved on since then. They continued to build small numbers of big guns, while the West concentrated on building big numbers of small guns. At sea, the Turks clung to their old tactics of ramming and boarding, but the ships they tried to board were now floating artillery batteries. On land, their heavy siege guns could not possibly keep up with the lighter guns of the West, which could be trundled into different positions relatively easily. The crunch came with the Christian victory at Vienna in 1683. The Turks had directed their heavy guns at the city, and could not move them round in time to tackle a large relief army that came charging out of the Vienna Woods.

Well into the eighteenth century, contemporary observers were noting how little Ottoman tactics had changed since the days of Suleyman the Magnificent. In his book *The Military Revolution*, Geoffrey Parker quotes the Maréchal de Saxe's comments in 1732: 'It is hard for one nation to learn from another, either from pride, idleness or stupidity. Inventions take a long time to be accepted (and sometimes, even though everyone accepts their usefulness, in spite of everything they are abandoned in favour of tradition and routine). ... The Turks today are in this situation. It is not valour, numbers or wealth that they lack; it is order, discipline and technique.'

In Britain, warships such as HMS *Victory* – which was to become Nelson's famous flagship at Trafalgar – were now being produced. *Victory* had a crew of 850 men and boys and 100 guns, each capable of firing more than once every two minutes. Ships like this, according to Simon Schaffer, were industrialized 'killing machines'.

'Making a large eighteenth-century warship needed more than 2,000 oak trees,' he says. 'Each rope of varying thickness needed to be spun from flax and the guns themselves had to be bored to very precise tolerances. So these were boats that on their own were the largest industrial enterprises of the eighteenth century – they outclassed any land-based factory. And running mechanical systems like this became the crucial site during the high point of the Industrial Revolution for training, for production and for the mass disciplining of a huge workforce.'

Admiralty-controlled dockyards at Portsmouth, Devonport and Chatham became increasingly like production lines. The old pit-saws, which had relied on the extremely exhausting labour of two very skilled sawyers, were replaced by steam-powered cutting machines. Work that had been done by a hundred skilled men could now be done at speed by ten relatively unskilled labourers. With the same efficiency applied to all areas of shipbuilding, precision engineering of standardized, replaceable parts became a reality.

When Nelson signalled ENGLAND EXPECTS THAT EVERY MAN WILL
DO HIS DUTY at the Battle of Trafalgar in 1805, the sweating labourers in
the dockyard back home may have been the last thing on his mind. But if
it hadn't been for them, such ships as the *Victory* would not have been
able to keep fighting battles and coming back for more.

'Britain's victory in the Napoleonic war owed less to the bulldog spirit,
and far more to technology and taxes,' says Simon Schaffer. 'The extraordinarily efficient British tax system, which relied on the knowledge of
the whole British economy, meant that the British government could raise
vast quantities of cash, both to pay foreign armies and also to build its own
war machine. And the technology that counted was naval technology.

'First of all, the science and technique of navigation which let British
mariners sail efficiently and rapidly across the world's oceans, but even
more importantly the standardized and efficient managerial system of the

Nelson receives his fatal
wound at the Battle of
Trafalgar, 1805. Tales of such
individual heroics have
tended to mask the more
mundane reasons for the
British victory over Napoleon.

naval dockyards and the ships themselves, which meant they could be re-equipped for sea extraordinarily fast, something which mattered a great deal during the maritime war against the French. So by 1815, with British maritime supremacy established, the nation emerged as the world's greatest colonial, imperial and economic power.'

The old days of Samuel Pepys, when the navy could not always even afford to pay its sailors, were clearly over. So, too, were the days of navigating by guess or by God. Now, if ships were lost at sea, it would not be simply because someone got their sums wrong. This had not always been the case, as Pepys himself experienced during a voyage to Tangiers in 1683. He noted: 'It is most plain, from the confusion all these people are in, how to make good their reckonings, even each man's with itself, and the nonsensical arguments they would make use of to do it, and disorder they are in about it, that it is by God's Almighty Providence and great chance, and the wideness of the sea, that there are not a great many more misfortunes and ill chances in navigation than there are.'

Everyone had their own way of working out where they were, once out of sight of land. Islamic sailors used 'rutters', which were poems that captains learnt by heart. These were practical reminders of methods of navigation, ranging from observations of the stars to tasting the water to see how salty it was. They were fine in familiar waters – but little use in uncharted territory. British sailors favoured 'dead reckoning', calculating their speed by throwing a line weighted by a piece of log overboard, and noting how long it took to get from one end of the ship to the other. This was then built into a complicated calculation involving the effect of ocean currents and changing winds, the position of the stars, and the time measured by a sandglass or pocket watch.

John Harrison's first chronometer, H1.

Sailing along a line of latitude was relatively easy: this was the method by which Columbus had reached America in 1492. All that was needed was an astrolabe to measure the height of the sun at noon. For this reason, some lines of latitude turned into shipping highways – not very helpful at times of fierce trade wars. Measuring longitude was more problematic. For every degree of longitude travelled, there will be a difference of four minutes of time, but this information is of little use if no accurate clocks are available. Traditional pendulum clocks were no use on board ship, due to the rolling motion, and changes in temperature and gravity. Added to this, while the difference of time remains constant, the difference in distance does not. Longitude lines converge at either pole, widening out towards the Equator.

At the very least, miscalculating a ship's position could mean patience-stretching extra days at sea. This was not something to be taken lightly on a long voyage, when scurvy and mutiny were equally ever-present threats. Most fatally, of course, getting the longitude wrong led to shipwreck. Admiral Sir Cloudesley Shovell and 2,000 sailors lost their lives after their fleet was wrecked on a squally September night in 1707. Due to incompetent navigation, they had thought they were off the coast of France instead of among the notoriously treacherous rocks of the Isles of Scilly. The needless loss of the Commander-in-Chief of the British Fleet in such circumstances at last prompted action. In 1714, an Act of Parliament offered a reward of £20,000 to anyone who could successfully produce a sea-going device to measure longitude.

This painting of John Harrison now hangs in the Old Royal Observatory — official recognition at last.

The size of the reward showed how urgent the problem was – and it also attracted a wide variety of eccentric solutions. In the end, though, the indefatigable efforts of John Harrison, a Yorkshire carpenter and self-taught clock-maker, produced a clock which could tell the time accurately at sea. This meant that a captain could compare the time on board ship with the time at his home port, and thus work out the longitude.

Harrison had been just twenty-one when the award was announced, and he spent a lifetime refining his ideas from sketches into working models. H1 – his first chronometer – was a large and cumbersome clock. By the time he reached his fourth prototype, H4, it had shrunk to the size of a large watch. He wrote: 'I think I may make bold to say that there is neither any other Mechanism or Mathematical thing in the World that is more beautiful or curious in texture than this my watch or Time-keeper for the Longitude.'

The device proved itself magnificently on a trial journey to Jamaica, but the Board of Longitude were reluctant to award him the prize. Some were themselves working on other ways of measuring longitude – and there could also have been an element of snobbery at this upstart Yorkshireman. They gave him a measly £2,500, and told him his device needed further trials. It was only after Harrison enlisted the help of King George III himself that he was finally granted the money. A deeply embittered man, he wrote to the Board: 'I hope I am the first, and for my country's sake, shall be the last that suffers from pinning my faith on an English Act of Parliament.'

In fact, however little they may have appeared to rate his ideas during his lifetime, the government was eventually to pay him the highest compliment by equipping the entire British fleet with Harrison-style chronometers. This was made possible by the way his invention was taken up and adapted for mass production by skilled watchmakers like John Arnold. While Harrison had laboured throughout his lifetime to produce five chronometers, John Arnold finished several hundred. His secret was to farm out routine work, leaving the finer adjustments for himself. He was also a skilled self-publicist, having made his name in his early twenties by presenting King George III with a half-inch-diameter miniature watch mounted on a ring. It is the story of Wedgwood once more.

The role of the hard-headed John Arnold, and others like him, in turning Harrison's ideas into practical reality foreshadows the role of Matthew Boulton in helping James Watt market his steam engines. As we saw in Chapter Two, the opportunities of 'networking' afforded by the burgeoning variety of clubs in Britain was vital: without this kind of collaboration, Britain would have been little more than an ideas shop, and the initiative would have moved elsewhere. Harrison was typical of the kind of characters who people the story of the Industrial Revolution in Britain: a rugged and determined individualist, who had good ideas but little notion of how to make money from them. He had the inventive genius: others had the entrepreneurial genius. Without this, his name would probably not be remembered today.

Among Harrison's supporters had been members of the Royal Society, which received its charter in 1660. This august body named among its members Isaac Newton, Robert Boyle and Christopher Wren. Its aim was to promote the 'useful arts', such as the work of navigators and engineers, as well as academic scientists. At a time of intense scientific activity, it was organizations such as this that provided an ideal meeting place for some of the most inventive thinkers of the age. In this clubbish atmosphere anyone could air their views, free from government intervention. This generated what has become known as the scientific revolution of the seventeenth century. However – as had been proved in Holland – a scientific revolution does not necessarily produce an industrial revolution. What was needed was the marriage of science and commerce.

Understandably, history textbooks tend to prefer to attach one name to an invention – but, in reality, many of the great breakthroughs involved a whole chain of people. For example, Boyle's theoretical interest in the phenomenon of atmospheric pressure produced a vacuum pump. This was made into a practical machine by Newcomen, an engineer, and eventually became a vital part of the engine that powered the *Rocket*. Inventions may have been protected for a limited time by patent, but ideas were patent-free. The kind of excitement that drew huge crowds to scientific lectures and exhibitions was a vital factor in progress. Wordsworth's words about the French Revolution: 'Bliss was it in that dawn to be alive' could equally well be applied to the scientific revolution. There was a real sense that they were pushing back the frontiers of knowledge.

As Simon Schaffer explains: 'The knowledge-making system of seventeenth-century England had a very powerful ideological warrant laid down by Francis Bacon, the Lord Chancellor in the 1610s and 1620s: "Many shall travel and knowledge will be increased." That's the slogan of his work, and on the frontispiece of his great books on the improvement of the sciences you see a picture of the pillars of Hercules, the straits between the Mediterranean and the Atlantic. You see ships sailing away from the known to the unknown world and then bringing back goods, commodities, facts, marvels, wonders … things of, as Bacon said, "light and profit".'

This vision of the world as a giant exotic pond just waiting for British ships to plunder was reinforced by a whole series of practical inventions that could make sailors feel a little more secure at sea. Apart from the chronometer, there were increasingly reliable sextants and compasses backed up by Edmund Halley's maps showing magnetic north.

Captain James Cook tested a Harrison chronometer on one of his voyages to the Pacific Ocean – an excellent illustration of the way science and exploration were combined in his journeys. Before his travels, the Pacific Ocean had been virtually uncharted, although there had been rumours of a large southern continent called Terra Australis Nondum Cognita (the Southern Land Not Yet Known), ever since Magellan's crossing of the Pacific in 1520. As is well known, Cook produced detailed maps of part of the coast of Australia, and all of New Zealand (once thought to be attached to Antarctica). Equally well known is Cook's sad fate, on his third voyage, where he was stabbed and killed in a struggle on Hawaii. However, he had left a lasting legacy of meticulously drawn charts, besides opening vast swathes of land for British colonization. The speed with which this happened – within three decades of Cook's first visit to the South Seas – shows just how eager the British were to expand at this period.

The idea for Cook's first and most famous voyage, in the *Endeavour* in 1786, had come from the Royal Society, who wanted to take accurate astronomical observations of Venus from the South Pacific. It was funded by the Admiralty, who were secretly keen for an opportunity to search for the Great Southern Continent. Meanwhile, the botanist Joseph Banks had seen the expedition as an ideal chance for a bit of specimen-collecting – which he did so successfully that Botany Bay in Australia was named after his efforts. Ironically, the fact that this area was later to become an infamous dumping ground for British convicts was largely due to Banks' enthusiastic descriptions of its attractions.

Captain Cook had started his seagoing life as an apprentice to a firm of Whitby coal-shippers, so when it came to choosing a ship for his voyage he chose a Whitby collier. This sturdy boat with its shallow draught was normally used only to carry that great English commodity, coal, between Newcastle and the Thames in winter. However, it was later to prove its worth when it was spiked by a bit of coral on the Great Barrier Reef. Despite being badly holed, it could be sailed off the reef when the tide turned, and mended on dry land.

The *Endeavour* was adapted for its new role in Deptford Royal Dockyard, where it was loaded up with food, livestock (to provide fresh meat) and ammunition. It had ten carriage guns and twelve swivel guns for self-defence, and scientific instruments including a portable observatory. Joseph Banks, together with his collecting equipment, a couple of dogs, and his team of seven took some loading. His entourage included a secretary and two paid artists – Alexander Buchan and Sydney Parkinson – who had been hired to draw scenic views and natural history specimens.

It was largely thanks to Banks, an enthusiastic and wealthy twenty-five-year-old, that the natural landscape they passed through was so well

A French map of 1739 showing the extent to which Cook was sailing into uncharted territory. *Nouvelle Zelande* (New Zealand) is shown attached to Antarctica.

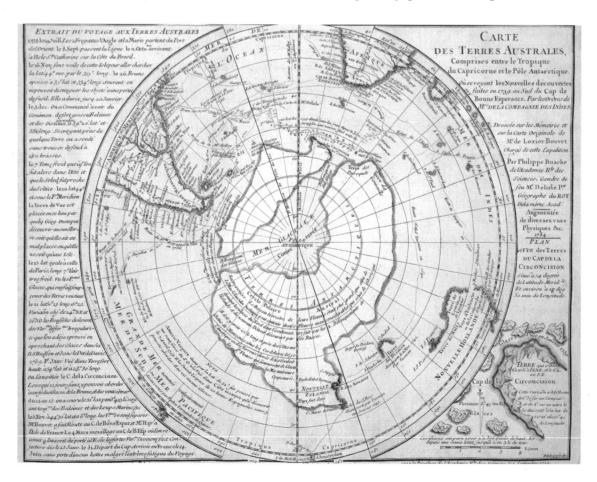

documented. Having succeeded to his family estates in Lincolnshire four years beforehand, he saw this voyage as an ideal opportunity to indulge his passion for botany and zoology. As Simon Schaffer puts it: 'Everyone he could compare himself with had been on the Grand Tour around Europe, so to trump them – and he said this explicitly – he went on the Grand Tour to Tahiti.'

When the *Endeavour* returned, after a three-year voyage, it had on board 30,000 specimens, representing some 3,000 species of which 1,600 were wholly new to science. These were not merely of theoretical, scientific interest – many were potentially of enormous practical use. Banks himself went on to become the first director of the Royal Gardens at Kew, an institution that became dedicated to the search for useful plants. Like so many of the great collections and museums of the time, conquering and making use of nature became a major concern.

Increasingly, voyages of exploration had a Kew connection. The infamous mutiny on the *Bounty* in 1791, for example, was at least partly prompted by a green, warty plant called the breadfruit. The plant is native to the western Pacific, where the seedless fruits are an important source of carbohydrate. Captain William Bligh's brief was to ship 1,000 breadfruit trees from Tahiti to the West Indies, as well as to take plants back to Kew. The story goes that the sailors wanted to drink water reserved for precious breadfruit seedlings; when Captain Bligh – mindful of his mission – refused, they mutinied. Among those who died after being cast adrift in an open boat was a Kew gardener.

Portrait of Sir Joseph Banks by Benjamin West, 1773. Banks is shown wrapped in a Maori cloak with trophies of a canoe paddle and a Tahitian headdress.

Kew spawned look-alike botanic gardens in far-flung parts of the empire, with acclimatization plots for new crops. As the eighteenth century turned into the nineteenth, it played an increasingly vital role in making life bearable for expatriates living in colonial outposts – and in developing industry. Two examples illustrate this: the introduction of quinine to help beat malaria in India, and rubber into tropical Asia. Both plants are native to South America and, in both cases, they reached their new destinations via Kew Gardens.

Engraving showing the transplantation of the breadfruit trees from Otaheite (Tahiti) – part of the chain of events which led to the Mutiny on the Bounty.

Shifting economically useful plants across the globe became only part of the complex network of trade routes developed by British merchant ships. At the hub of this process – as we saw in the first chapter – was the flourishing port of Liverpool. Some indication of the variety of goods involved comes from meticulous weekly records kept by the Liverpool Corn Exchange. These were then faithfully reproduced in the *Liverpool Chronicle*. In the week ending 18 September 1830, for instance, the *Chronicle* listed 19,340 bags of cotton wool, 1,004 casks of rum, 2,753 cow and ox hides, ninety-seven tons of hemp, 1175 bags of rice from India – and forty elephant teeth from Africa. Plus varying quantities of sugar, molasses, coffee, cocoa, spices, cochineal, indigo, olive oil, tobacco and tar.

The secret of success was to develop circular trading routes. The Ottomans, for instance, had traded in straight lines. Ships brought goods back to fill the bazaars, but had little to offer in exchange. In the end, this meant spending out for very little return. Europeans, by contrast, filled and emptied ships at every port of call – and each time, they made a profit. Of course, to their eternal shame, the commodity that was a vital element in this trading circle up until the mid nineteenth century were slaves. Between 1600 and 1850, ten million people were taken by force from their homes and made to work, without any reward, in the most appalling conditions, for the benefit of the European economy. It may have been of little comfort to them as they slaved for their new masters, but their labour on the cotton and sugar plantations was an essential part of the trading equation.

A vital factor in the spread of European culture across the globe, particularly to North America, was the growing number of emigrants forced through poverty or religious persecution to look for a better future abroad. The process had started during the 1630s, when some 20,000 people left Britain for New England. Whole communities had set up agricultural colonies, working the land with their own labour and soon becoming independent of the mother country. Success bred success, although the hardships and dangers of the Atlantic crossing were a major deterrent.

This problem in its turn was considerably lessened by the advent of the steam age. The first Atlantic crossing by steamship was in 1819, and in 1838 Brunel's wonder of the age, the SS *Great Britain*, arrived in New York harbour. No longer dependent on wind or tide, crossings were now faster and safer. Steamships also meant that – even after gaining its independence – the United States kept in touch with the mother country. It is arguable that it is because of steam that we can talk about 'Western culture' at all.

By 1850, there was no question but that the future was in the hands of the people with the steam engines. The all-powerful sultans, retreating behind the shrinking frontiers of the once-glorious Ottoman Empire, were out of the race. Centralized power, it seems, had simply stifled, rather than encouraged innovation. The Dutch had been so successful at teaching others how to make money and rule the waves in the first part of the seventeenth century that they, too, had been left behind. Britain now seemed to be in the lead – but how long would this last? And why had all the vital ingredients been available to Europeans at just the right time? Weren't there other civilizations that might have developed a global culture – such as China, for instance? To answer some of these questions, we need to travel backwards in time once again – this time, taking the 500-year perspective.

Chapter Four

THE HEAVENLY MACHINE

When Alan Macfarlane was seventeen, he went on a school trip to Fountains Abbey in Yorkshire. Looking out over the ruins, his teacher said: 'Boys, this is the origin of the modern world, the capitalist revolution, the Industrial Revolution, it's all here.' The idea that the great monastic orders had been a crucial influence in the creation of industrial society has intrigued him ever since.

Accordingly, Alan Macfarlane began this 500-year overview of the origins of the Industrial Revolution by visiting a Benedictine monastery. Pluscarden Abbey was flourishing in 1350 and continues to this day – one of the few original working Benedictine monasteries that are still left in Britain.

Like most monasteries, Pluscarden is set in beautiful surroundings, tucked beneath the wooded hills of Moray in Scotland. It is a refuge of calm and tranquillity for the twenty-eight monks who live there. Their day begins at 4.45 am when they gather for matins and lauds. In the summer it is already light but, in the winter, dawn is five hours away. It is the first of seven acts of communal worship that form the central framework of their daily life. Seven times a day a bell rings. Seven times a day they walk through the cloisters in their long white habits to the choir, where they begin their Gregorian chants. This is the outward manifestation of a strict set of rules laid down by St Benedict. He had conceived of a way of life that enabled initiates to escape the doubts and fluctuations of worldly life by combining prayer, work and study in a set routine. In *The Rule of St Benedict*, he states: 'Idleness is the enemy of the soul. For this reason the brethren should be occupied at certain times in manual labour and at other times in sacred reading.'

Father Giles, the Abbey's Prior, explains the Benedictine philosophy succinctly: 'It's a balanced life: something for the head, something for the heart, something for the hands, and it's done in community, so everybody is supporting everyone else.'

Alan Macfarlane was interested in the Benedictine tradition of using wit and ingenuity to design labour-saving mechanical devices. Because they had to do all their own farm work, without having serfs to do the laborious pounding and grinding, they would have had no time for prayer unless they could apply their intelligence to think of ways of improving their lot. As he says: 'This is what makes them different from any other mandarin class, who can let the peasants do what they like, as long as they produce the goods.'

Father Giles thinks many of those traditions continue. 'Monks tend to be, in my experience, lateral thinkers,' he says. 'If you tell a monk to go and feed the pigs, he will tend to say to himself: "Well, life is a bit busy. How can I improve on this? How can I think of a way of feeding the pigs which will speed things up, or make it a little less complicated?"

'While all the solutions produced by monks may not be always those that would appeal to the conventional mind, they usually work, and I have seen some very strange, but effective, solutions to problems and I'm sure that part of the monastic vocation is clearly to contrapt, to produce contraptions. Again, we look at ancient authors and they were full of ideas of how to do things, measuring this or that, or driving this or that. They were pioneers in lots of things and in some ways still are.'

By 1350 over 1 per cent of the English population lived in monasteries. They were there to provide not just spiritual sustenance, but also a more practical, down-to-earth service for the community. There were no

The monks of Pluscarden Abbey continue the Benedictine tradition of dividing their day between four and a half hours of worship and four and a half hours of labour, reading and chores. An awareness of time is critical to such a finely balanced life.

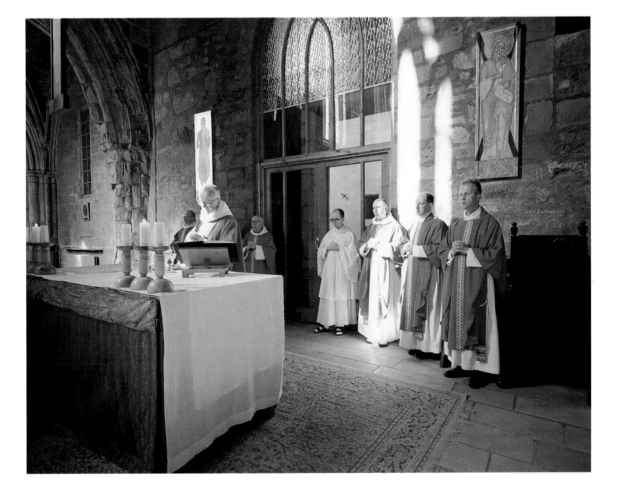

hospitals or hotel chains for people to stay in. If you were sick or needed a bed for a night, you went to a monastery.

In the Middle Ages monks became experts in metal-smelting, brewing, and harnessing water power for milling. Even during prayer, their day was dominated by two technologies whose impact is less obvious: the sound of the bell marking the passage of time, and the sight of light streaming through stained-glass windows.

The central idea in this chapter is that the measurement of time with mechanical clocks and the transmission of light through glass not only improved monastic life, but also played an important role in enabling industrial civilization to emerge in the West. The evolution of these critical technologies over the next few centuries laid the foundations for the scientific revolution. Their significance extends much further than the practical applications of making instruments and scientific apparatus. These inventions would gradually change people's perception of time and space. Although they may not have been aware of it, Europeans began to live their lives according to a more precise set of mathematical rules.

A fifteenth-century monk copies manuscripts beneath stained glass windows.

Britain at the beginning of this period was an island outpost of little consequence. Other parts of western Eurasia looked much more promising. Venice and Constantinople both looked as though they might be destined to dominate the globe. Yet it was the great Eastern cities of Kyoto and Beijing that were the cosmopolitan centres. China was the 'Middle Kingdom', the centre of the world – and its civilization far ahead of that of anyone else.

The Silk Road between Europe and Asia was busy. Missionaries, merchants and envoys could travel anywhere they wanted from the far west of Europe to the east coast of China. Provided they paid import duty on their goods, anyone was free to travel. So, in theory, conditions were right for a vigorous diffusion of ideas and technologies. In practice, in the first half of this 500-year period, the great Middle Kingdom felt there was very little of interest to learn from the barbaric corners of Europe; and in the second half, the East became rather impatient with Western missionary zeal. So technology in the two parts of the Eurasian landmass followed very different paths.

In the first three chapters, we have looked at a wide variety of technologies in a small time frame. Now, as we widen the historical perspective, our technological focus becomes narrower. Could developments in glass- and clock-making help to solve the riddle of why industrialization happened in Europe first, rather than in the eastern part of Eurasia, which was more advanced in almost every way in 1350?

The story starts with the invention of the mechanical clock. Many pieces of this puzzle are missing. It is not even entirely clear what motivated the first clock-makers to build such machines. Were they trying to keep track of time, or did they have grander aspirations to mimic the movement of heavenly bodies in the night sky? Did a need for a synchronized society lead to the invention of the mechanical clock, or did the introduction of the mechanical clock develop into an obsession with time-keeping?

In classical civilizations the time of day was measured using sundials or water clocks. These devices worked well in sunny climates but, when the weather was cloudy or cold, sundials were useless and water clocks froze. So neither were particularly well suited to the north European climate.

The exact date the mechanical clock first appeared in Europe is uncertain. By 1350 we know that a clock tower with an astronomical dial had been installed in Norwich Cathedral, and that Richard of Wallingford's complex astronomical clock at St Albans was half-way through construction. But there were probably earlier mechanical clocks dating back to the end of the thirteenth century. (There is no direct evidence because the cogs, fly-wheels and other metal parts from these old clocks would have been stripped out and re-used – a recurring problem in industrial archaeology.) The question remains: why were these machines built and where did this great intellectual leap of mechanical clockwork come from? In addition to telling the time, these clocks displayed a moving map of the heavens. Some historians believe that the original invention had more to do with taking astronomical measurements than the need to know the time.

In a book called *Heavenly Clockwork*, a group of scholars of Chinese history led by Joseph Needham argued that the great Chinese astronomical clocks from the turn of the first millennium were the forgotten origins of clockwork in Europe. As they put it: 'The mechanical clock is nought but a fallen angel from the world of astronomy!'

The most elaborate of these astronomical devices was the Su Sung clock, which was completed at the end of the eleventh century. This was a huge machine as big as a two-storey house. It was powered by a large water-wheel. As each bucket on the wheel filled with water, it tripped a lever that brought the next bucket into position. It was a kind of escapement mechanism that converted a continuous motion into separate, discontinuous steps. A set of cogs and vertical drive shafts moved a series of rings, called armillary spheres, which represented the paths of the sun, the moon and various stars that were important in the Chinese calendar.

By lining up the sights on a star, astronomers could confirm the accuracy of the clock. Accuracy was important because this clock was used as a celestial decision-maker for the emperor. Astronomy and astrology were as one, so minute changes in the cosmos could determine whether the emperor slept with the empress or one of his concubines.

'Chinese culture was very interested in time indeed,' explains Christopher Cullen. 'One of the central functions of the Imperial State from the beginning of the Chinese Empire was to provide an accurate calendar. And by calendar I mean not just the days or the equivalent of the week or the month, but an increasingly detailed scheme that told you what the cosmos would be doing at any instant – what the moon and the sun would be up to – and so on. This was not just for the purpose of contemplation and seeking after knowledge, but because the Chinese scheme of how you ought to plan your life very much laid stress on doing things at the right time. If you didn't do a ritual at the right time, if you didn't bring up medical

This cutaway reconstruction of the Su Song clock shows the technical sophistication of Chinese craftsmen two centuries before the first mechanical clocks were built in Europe. The puzzle is why these skills were lost. Scholars have tried to build models of the clock from Su Song's building instructions to establish how it worked.

treatment at the right time, if you got married at the wrong time, things would go badly awry. So exactly at what moment things should be done was very important in China.'

The imperial astronomers were meant to report independently to the emperor, but they were so terrified of presenting conflicting data they often colluded before making their reports. As David Landes explains in his book, *Revolution in Time*: 'If the astronomers found an anomaly, the armillary sphere could be adjusted and the calendar corrected. The important thing was the appearance of knowledge, duly certified to the ruler by the court astronomers and proclaimed by him to the people. The criterion, in other words, was political rather than scientific.'

This leads us back to the question of the origins of the European mechanical clock. Did a thirteenth- or fourteenth-century craftsman piece together the mechanism based on descriptions from the East or was it invented independently? Joseph Needham and his colleagues argue that the Chinese astronomical clocks were the forerunners of the European mechanical clock. However, the 200-year gap before the idea materialized in the West and the type of clockwork mechanism developed in Europe make this transition seem a little unlikely. Even if the idea of clockwork did spread from the East, the evolution of this technology followed extraordinarily different paths in the two parts of Eurasia.

David Landes' explanation in *Revolution in Time* seems more plausible. He thinks that the building of the mechanical clock in Europe was a response to the need to measure time. He points to the frequent references to the cost of cathedral clock repairs by the end of the thirteenth century and concludes that the complex astronomical clocks of Richard of Wallingford and Dondi of Padua were third- or fourth-generation devices that were based on a crucial intellectual leap in Europe. Someone came up with the idea of using falling weights to drive an escapement mechanism that converted the back-and-forth motion of a rotating bar into a step-by-step division of time. As he sums it up: 'The clock did not create an interest in time measurement; the interest in time measurement led to the clock.'

But where did this interest come from? In the countryside, where nine out of ten Europeans lived, there was little need to know the time of day beyond the natural rhythm of sunrise and sunset. In the towns, knowing the time could help traders and craftsmen organise their day, particularly when they arranged to meet. But the institution with the most pressing demand for accurate time-keeping was the monastery.

The Benedictine rule meant that monks had always to be acutely aware of time. They needed to be woken before daybreak and summoned from the vegetable patch before vespers. The children's song 'Frère Jacques' immortalizes a brother's fear of not waking to ring the bells to call the monks to matins.

Frère Jacques, Frère Jacques,
Dormez-vous? Dormez vous?
Sonnez les matines, sonnez les matines,
Ding, ding, dong; ding, ding, dong.

The clock of the Church of Our Lady in Nuremberg is a fine example of a Gothic time pageant. Like many cities in medieval Europe, Nuremberg wanted to demonstrate its importance with the size and complexity of its mechanical clocks.

The direct benefits of introducing clocks into monasteries are obvious, but being ruled by time may have had a more far-reaching effect as Alan Macfarlane suggests: 'What the Benedictines did was to enclose space and time physically in their architecture, socially in their social organization, and then divide it all up into tiny bits, so in a sense they were a living clock, a kind of physical social clock in their order.'

The holy calling of a fourteenth-century monk may seem to have little to do with the origins of the Industrial Revolution, but religious brothers had one thing in common with workers toiling in cotton mills. Although they lived five centuries apart, they both understood the consequences of ignoring the discipline of time. The regular rhythm of the demands of God was a foretaste of the more strident stroke of the Machine Age.

Thus the daily cycle of monastic life was a precursor of a more regulated working life that would evolve in Europe over the next few centuries. It is a strange paradox that regular prayer for the welfare of souls in eternity created temporal order in the minds of men, which in turn gave rise to a state of mind that would eventually underscore capitalist civilization.

Yet why was this obsession with time confined to European monasticism? Buddhism and Islam both had a tradition of regular daily worship. Wouldn't they have benefited from mechanical clocks in their cultures? The Islamic calls to prayer are between sunrise and sunset, so perhaps the passage of the sun provided the necessary information. In the case of Buddhism, long periods of meditation are important, but their timing is not so crucial.

Perhaps there were other reasons connected to the degree of autonomy enjoyed by the religion. Buddhism came into civilizations that were already heavily populated and the religion was subordinate to the political powers; whereas the Benedictine orders came into the world after the crushing of the Roman Empire, so they were not subjected to the same kind of political domination.

By the end of the fourteenth century, the fascination with clockwork was spreading rapidly across Europe. Building a clock tower became a matter of civic pride. Every town wanted one, the more elaborate and costly the better. The passage of time eventually turned into a public spectacle with theatrical displays of gilded figures striking the hour. These great clocks were the technological sensation of their time, but as clocks became more widespread there was a more profound impact. Citizens in Europe became aware of the time of day and their lives became increasingly organized.

The Forbidden City was the imperial palace complex where the most senior scholar-officials were invited for audiences with the Emperor. They often arrived hours before dawn and waited in ante-rooms. During the night, the only men allowed within the palace's private chambers were eunuchs.

In China no public clocks were built in the towns, even though there were craftsmen capable of building such machines two centuries before the first European clocks appeared. This unfulfilled potential is a recurring puzzle in the history of Chinese technology. Christopher Cullen, who prefers to ask why things happened in Europe rather than why they didn't happen in China, offers this explanation: 'The idea of having this wonderful exhibition of mechanical skill – "They've got one in Nuremberg, so we must have one here" – Chinese towns don't go in for that,' he says. 'This makes me think that the story of the mechanical clock may not at first be so much about the desire for public time (because the Chinese have got publicly available time too); but something to do with the display of the particular skills involved in making clocks. So I think that we might have to look at why making clever mechanical devices that do public tricks that have some utility is something that people admire in Europe.'

Another explanation revolves around this concept of public time, which did not exist in China. In a sense time, like space, was a commodity owned by the emperor. In Beijing the drum and bell towers (which still exist today) used to sound the hours and performed a function that at first appears similar to a clock tower in Europe. But perversely, they operated only during the night between sunset and sunrise. Why, you might wonder, should bells and drums sound at night? Surely the emperor's subjects

would all be asleep? The answer is that anyone needing an audience in the Forbidden City had to arrive hours before dawn to begin their long journey through the layers of officialdom. They needed the alarm calls to avoid being late for the emperor. No one else's time mattered. It did not belong to them. The important thing was to ensure the emperor never had to wait – that, by definition, would be a waste of time.

This difference in philosophy may also help explain the different attitude to clockwork in the East and West. In China the clock was an important instrument for taking astronomical (that is, astrological) measurements that enabled the emperor and his court to make decisions about the future. In Europe, by contrast, the clock had a more immediate significance. It was an instrument for synchronizing actions, rather than making predictions.

Joel Mokyr describes how the arrival of the clock changed Europe: 'Within a few decades every town in Europe had a clock tower that gave a clock to anybody who wanted to look. And this was something that set Europe apart from other societies that tried to measure time. It's not just that they were interested, but that it was democratic. It wasn't the emperor's time or the king's time or the duke's time; this was time that everybody could look at and know what time it was. From an economic point of view this was a huge step forward because a lot of economic activity, as well as social activity, requires coordination.

'If you and I decide to have lunch tomorrow and we have lunch at 12.30, it's presumed that 12.30 for you is 12.30 for me; so we actually touch base. But if we make an appointment in the middle of the day, when the sun is at the top of the sky, you may miss by half an hour, and that makes coordination more difficult to do.'

Simon Schaffer thinks this growing awareness of personal time is critical. 'I see a very strong relationship, which emerges between the 1300s and the 1500s, between mechanical clocks and an individualization or privatization of time,' he says. 'It is important to look away from the monastic kind of coordination to exactly this idea of arranging a meeting with another individual, telling other people what to do and measuring what they are doing.'

The idea of time as a precious commodity, that could be spent, saved or wasted, started to cause friction in the relationship between employers and their workers. In the countryside, peasants still sowed and ploughed as they had always done, from sunrise to sunset. In textile towns such as Bruges or Ghent, however, work bells started to insinuate themselves into the daily routine. Whether these were housed in church clock towers or were private bells owned by employers, they were equally resented – especially by people doing piece-work at home. Since out-workers were paid by results, they could not see why it mattered when they started and stopped work.

The Black Death of 1347–50 substantially reduced the available workforce and gave the surviving workers new political muscle. At Thérouanne in 1367, the Church authorities agreed to silence the workers' bell after protests. However, despite several revolts elsewhere, the bells generally rang on. Part of the problem was mistrust, a suspicion that the employer might somehow be 'fixing' the bells to their advantage. This may have been an early example of an urban myth because there is little evidence that such 'fixing' actually happened.

Suspicion lessened once clock towers had clock faces as well as bells. This meant that when they chimed every quarter of an hour employer and employee could both check the time. The clock was no longer the enemy of the people; it was an independent gauge of the quantity of work completed.

Lewis Mumford, in *Technics and Civilization*, describes the enormous impact of clocks in Europe. He wrote:

The regular striking of bells brought a new regularity into the life of the workman and the merchant. The bells of the clock tower almost defined urban existence. Time-keeping passed into time-serving and time-accounting and time-rationing. As this took place, Eternity ceased gradually to serve as the measure and focus of human actions. The clock, not the steam engine, is the key machine of the modern industrial age. For every phase of its development the clock is both the outstanding fact and typical symbol of the machine: even today no other machine is so ubiquitous.

The clock has another claim over the steam engine as the ultimate symbol of the industrial age. The precision engineering required to assemble and adjust delicately balanced cogs and wheels made it a vital precursor to the steam engine. This technology became more and more sophisticated, as portable clocks and watches became popular. A recurring theme of modernization is the way demand became the mother of invention. A ready market meant manufacturers experimented with division of labour to produce cheap, accurate watches.

These individual timepieces – no longer the preserve of the moneyed classes – gave everyone control over how they spent their time. Many historians have highlighted the importance of the hard-working, driven individual in the growth of the Industrial Revolution, and the watch was the tool that helped create this state of mind. As David Landes points out, a public clock is only any use if you can see or hear it. 'A chamber clock or watch is something very different: an ever-visible, ever-audible companion and monitor. A turning hand, specifically a minute hand (the hour hand turns so slowly as to seem still), is a measure of time used, time spent, time wasted, time lost. As such it was prod and key to personal achievement and productivity.'

Just as the mechanical clock revolutionized the way people organized their time, glass changed their perception of space and their outlook on the world. The story of how glass developed in the West but not in the East, has many parallels with the story of clockwork.

At Pluscarden Abbey the pattern of the monks' day may be ruled by the tick of the clock and the ring of the bell, but it is the transmission of light through the magnificent stained-glass windows that helps create the aura of sanctity that infuses the place. On summer mornings, during the celebration of mass, shafts of sunlight stream through the clear panes of glass that line the south side of the choir. When the monks step forward and lift the silver communion cup to their lips, a reflected glow baptizes each face with sunlight. As the day moves from dawn to dusk the stained-glass windows reflect the glory of God in each chapel and transept.

Many of Pluscarden's stained-glass windows have been made by the monks themselves over the last few decades, maintaining a tradition that goes back to medieval times. The origin of glass-making remains uncertain. It is an ancient skill, which probably appeared first in Egypt or Mesopotamia and then spread across most of Eurasia. The process is relatively simple, although it requires a lot of energy to melt the raw materials. In theory, glass can be made from heating sand alone. In practice, the temperature required is so high that potash or soda is added to reduce the melting point. A third ingredient, lime, was later introduced to stabilize the glass and prevent it from dissolving in water.

In the first century BC there was a breakthrough that created a new breed of craftsman: the glass blower. The origin of this craft is not known. Perhaps someone had noticed bubbles forming in molten glass or had carried out an idle experiment blowing through a hollow tube; but this magical trick allowed a new elegance and intricacy in glass objects. Generations of craftsmen were inspired by the way glass could be blown into spheres, drawn out into threads and welded together with invisible joints. These properties would later be exploited for making scientific instruments.

In *De Re Metallica*, a guide to technology first published in 1556, Georgius Agricola describes the art of glass-blowing:

When he blows through the pipe he blows as he would if inflating a bubble; he blows into the blow-pipe as often as it is necessary, removing it from his mouth to re-fill

In northern Europe clocks became the first household machines. This domestic clock was probably made in Germany in the fifteenth century.

An early glass-works showing the large kiln, from which the glass-blowers drew their molten glass. The engraving is from *De Re Metallica*, an illustrated textbook of medieval technology.

his cheeks, so that his breath does not draw the flames into his mouth. Then, twisting the lifted blow-pipe round his head in a circle, he makes a long glass, or moulds the same in a hollow copper mould, turning it round and round, then warming it again, blowing it and pressing it, he widens it into the shape of a cup or vessel, or of any other object he has in mind.

The revival of interest in glass began in the Middle Ages. The furnaces were often sited in wooded areas near monasteries. Acres of forest were felled to fuel the insatiable demand for glass from the cities of Europe. By the sixteenth century timber was becoming an increasingly scarce resource and there was competition between iron works and glass works for the limited supplies. An ironmaster from Sussex, jealous of the success of glass workers, had this message for them: 'Try another district farther removed from the Metropolis, if you must carry on your luxury craft; and in any case fell timber in some place where Sussex iron ore doesn't grow, and where oak trees are not wanted for the wooded halls of England. We think we may make shift to do without glass cups and goblets 'till enough cannons have been cast and balls to feed them. How if we have a turn as the favourite of Kings? In short, Gentlemen, 'tis time for you to trek.'

Glass had become a highly prized luxury throughout Europe. Venetian glass, which had the reputation as the finest in the world, was more sought after than silver or gold. One contemporary observed: 'It is a world to see in these our dais, wherein gold and silver most aboundeth, how that our gentilitie as loathing those metals (because of the plentie) do now generally choose rather the Venice glasses both for our wine and our beere than any of those metals or stone wherein before time we have beene accustomed to drink.'

The Venetians were so anxious to protect their glass-making secrets that they moved the manufacture to the island of Murano to prevent foreign spies gaining access. The penalties for passing on secrets to other countries were severe. In 1547 the Council of Venice added a new article to their Statute: 'If a workman carries his art abroad to the detriment of the Republic, an order to return will be sent to him. If he disobeys the order his next of kin will be imprisoned. If in spite of this he persists in living abroad, an emissary will be sent to kill him.'

With these thoughts in his head, Alan Macfarlane landed on the island of Murano. Here the tradition of glass-making continues, but nowadays the manufacturers compete with each other to encourage foreign visitors.

Venice is an interesting case history to examine because at the start of the 500 years covered by this chapter, it was at the peak of its power. By 1350 Venice was a highly successful trading state with a huge merchant fleet and a formidable navy. The canal system provided the perfect link to the sea, which was the fastest highway in the world. Exporting goods by sea (especially breakable ones like glass) was a lot quicker and safer than attempting bumpy road journeys across land.

Alan Macfarlane sees Venice as an example of a state which had many of the special qualities seen in successful modern societies. He thinks the secret of their success lies in the uneasy tension that existed between the different spheres of life. This gave Venice an advantage few other places enjoyed at this time. The State was not too powerful (it was one of the first great republics), so there was political freedom. It was also relatively free from the religious pressures of the papacy because it was an island. If the Catholic Church did try to intervene, the Venetians devised ingenious solutions to avoid conflict.

A good example was a Church ruling that made the borrowing and lending of money illegal. A commercial empire on the scale of Venice needed liquid capital, so its merchants had to find a way round this problem. They created the world's first Jewish ghetto as a money-

The Barovier Marriage Cup of 1445 is a hand-blown glass bowl made by one of the oldest Murano glass-working families. Murano glassware is renowned for the intricacy and delicacy of its craftsmanship.

laundering operation. The Jews were not allowed to mingle with Venetians outside this ghetto. The business was done within a small restricted area that used to be an iron foundry. (The word 'ghetto' means iron foundry and the word entered the language from this walled-off area of Venice.)

Shakespeare illustrates the hypocrisy implicit in this arrangement in Shylock's words to Antonio in *The Merchant of Venice*:

> *You call me misbeliever, cut-throat dog,*
> *And spit upon my Jewish gaberdine,*
> *And all for use of that which is mine own.*
> *Well then, it now appears you need my help;*
> *Go to then; you come to me, and you say,*
> *'Shylock, we would have moneys'. You say so –*
> *You that did void your rheum upon my beard*
> *And foot me as you spurn a stranger cur*
> *Over your threshold … .*

The scale of Venice's maritime business generated wealth that helped keep all the different interests separate. This combination of liberalism, egalitarianism and commercialism made it a vibrant, flourishing society. Yet by the time England was beginning to industrialize, three or four centuries later, Venice had faded away. So what happened?

Its key disadvantage was size. Venice was swallowed by the larger empires that emerged during this period. It also suffered from a lack of raw materials, in particular iron and coal; so the development of an 'iron age' was impossible. And finally, energy was in short supply – it had no fast-running rivers, little wind and no forests. Initially the raw materials were imported, but eventually the cost made it impractical, which is why the iron foundry eventually turned into a ghetto.

Venice carried on as a commercial port, and Murano glassware continued to be very popular in the banqueting halls of Europe. The high quality of Murano glass would later make it ideally suited for lens production, but Venice did not have the monopoly in glass-making. Large quantities of glass were being manufactured for very different reasons in the colder climate of northern Europe.

Window glass had been around since Roman times. By the Middle Ages it was being used to create the grand stained-glass windows of Gothic cathedrals. To produce different-coloured glass, metallic oxides were added: cobalt gave a dark blue, iron produced green and the different oxides of copper gave blue, ruby and other shades of green. While stained-glass windows were becoming widespread in churches, clear crown-glass windows were becoming increasingly common in public buildings.

Crown glass was produced by gathering a large blob of molten glass on the end of a blowpipe and blowing a sphere. An assistant created a small round hole by removing a disc of glass. Then, in a virtuoso display of red-hot juggling, the most skilled blower spun the hollow sphere faster and faster until the centrifugal forces suddenly flashed the sphere into a flat disc of glass. The circular sheets were relatively small and brittle. In the middle of each one was the raised bull's eye or crown that gave the glass its name. Although today they often adorn 'ye olde tea shoppes', the crowns used to be thrown away as scrap. Only small squares of glass could be cut from the rest of the sheet, so this process could not be used for making larger windows.

At first, glass was so precious that only public buildings had glass windows. The panes were removable so they could be put in storage if a building was left unoccupied for any time. Then gradually, as the cost declined, most urban houses had glass windows. By the time the *Rocket* made its journey in 1830, the crown-glass method of window manufacture had become almost obsolete. It was replaced by the bigger-scale hand-cylinder process that produced large sheets of glass.

Glass manufacture was an important industry in itself, but the real significance of the substance was the impact it had on modern living. Imagine living through the long cold winters of northern Europe without glass. Before glass, houses were dark, dirty places. It is not hard to see why early civilizations flourished in the warm climate of the eastern Mediterranean. Eating, thinking, scholarship and trade could be conducted outside or in light open rooms. Glass windows transformed indoor life in northern Europe. If a workshop had glass windows, the working day could be longer and productivity could be improved during cold weather. It meant that backward countries with wet miserable climates like England and Holland could at last start catching up. It was a new era of indoor civilization.

Glass not only lets in more light, but it makes every mote of dust visible. The enormous windows of seventeenth-century Dutch homes bathed the rooms with sunlight, leaving no dark corners to hide traces of dirt. This created a new hygienic environment that encouraged cleaning and turned it into an important ritual of everyday life. The floor, the pewter, the glass dome of the clock, even the windowpane itself, had to be cleaned.

Glass also had a more abstract effect on people's experience of the outside world. It literally created a window on the world, making it possible to see reality from a more defined perspective, within a frame. The image in the eye could be sharpened by another property of glass that would eventually revolutionize science and extend working life. This was the ability of glass to bend light and magnify objects.

The first spectacle lenses appeared at the end of the thirteenth century. These were for correcting long-sightedness, or presbyopia; lenses to correct short-sightedness, myopia, were not to appear for a further two centuries. Presbyopia was a common problem facing middle-aged people (just as it is today). It is caused by the hardening of the eye lens, which makes focusing on close objects impossible. As the problem gets worse, the only way of reading a book is to hold it further and further away, until eventually the words are no longer visible. The defect is easily corrected by placing a convex lens in front of the eye.

The puzzle is why it took so long to invent spectacles. As Joel Mokyr points out: 'The Romans had excellent glass-blowing facilities. They could have made lenses had they wanted to. They must have needed them, because the same physiological processes that cause presbyopia in us now must have been true for the Romans as well. They were literate, many of them read, many of them were fine craftsmen who needed to see small things, and yet they never developed eye-glasses. Now why?'

Joel Mokyr offers a possible explanation, which is that making decent spectacles requires more than glass-making skills. There was a need to understand the geometry and science of optics in order to produce accurate lenses. He thinks Islamic scientists such as Alhazen, who studied the reflection of light rays in curved mirrors and glass spheres, may have had an influence. There is no evidence that the person who first made spectacles over 200 years later had ever read Alhazen's texts, but the knowledge could have been passed on over the centuries.

Alan Macfarlane has a different explanation for the riddle of why the Romans never made spectacles. He argues that if you have educated slaves, you have no need for glasses as you get older. You simply tell your slave to read to you. Pliny would often have servants reading aloud to avoid wasting time. So as long as you had a younger slave or apprentice to read to you, there was no need for spectacles. This practice continued in churches and in monastic orders. Private, silent reading was a concept that developed much later in the West. One of the few places to maintain the tradition of reading aloud today is the Benedictine monastery. At Pluscarden, meals in the refectory are accompanied by reading aloud – feeding the mind as well as the body. During the course of the week a new story unfolds chapter by chapter.

The invention of spectacles may seem like a trivial aid to medieval living, but it doubled the working life of skilled craftsmen, particularly those who did fine jobs, such as instrument-makers, weavers or scribes. The additional years of human eyesight also had an impact on the revival of learning. Older, more experienced scholars were able to continue to read and write and contribute to intellectual life. By the fifteenth century, the invention of printing had created even more demand for eye-glasses. Proofreaders, typesetters, printers – they all needed glasses.

Although the highest-quality optical glass came from Venice, the art of precision lens grinding never developed there. Again this new technology evolved in northern Europe, particularly in The Netherlands. As we saw in Chapter Three, at the end of the sixteenth century Dutch opticians including Johann Lippersheim and Zacharias Jansen were producing extraordinarily accurate lenses, which would be used in different combinations to make the first telescopes and compound microscopes. By the turn of the next century the details of the craters of the moon and the eyes of a fly could be seen for the first time.

Lewis Mumford in *Technics and Civilization* highlights the far-reaching impact of these optical instruments. As he puts it: 'One invention increased the scope of the macrocosm; the other revealed the microcosm: between them, the naïve conceptions of space that the ordinary man carried around were completely upset: one might say that these two inventions, in terms of the new perspective, extended the vanishing point toward infinity and increased almost infinitely the plane of the foreground from which those lines had their point of origin.'

So what had happened between 1350 and 1600 that had made this new use of glass possible? A key factor is the growth of reliable knowledge – a definition of science – and the ability to think about objects and make them in a very precise way. Simon Schaffer emphasizes the importance of precision engineering to lens-making. 'By the seventeenth century lens-making was not merely a very sophisticated technology, it was the *most* precise, demanding technique of any, by four or five orders of magnitude,' he says. 'Grinding a perfect lens is so much more difficult and so much more time-consuming than almost anything else any European was doing.'

The revolution in science went hand in hand with the revolution in glass. Without glass, science could not have progressed. Imagine chemistry without glass: no test tubes, retorts or distillation flasks. Or physics: no thermometers, barometers or bell jars. Or medicine: no microscope slides, specimen containers or culture dishes.

No other material has such a rich combination of properties: it is transparent (allowing chemical reactions or biological specimens to be viewed); it is inert (so it can withstand corrosive chemicals); it becomes malleable when heated (so it can be blown into complex shapes); it is easily cleaned (so apparatus can be re-used for experiments); and it is strong (so vacuum experiments pumping air out of glass vessels are possible).

Without glass Galileo, Torricelli, Boyle and many other scientists could not have studied the relationship between temperature, pressure and the expansion of gases. And without this knowledge the construction of the *Rocket* two centuries later would have been impossible.

There was one other use of glass, which had a more elusive – and egocentric – effect on civilization. By coating a sheet of glass with a silver amalgam, the surface could be turned into a mirror. One of the highest achievements of the grand Venetian glass-makers was the production of mirrors. Initially they only appeared in the salons of the aristocracy, but eventually small hand-mirrors became common possessions. Lewis Mumford highlights the unexpected consequences of the use of mirrors:

For perhaps the first time, except for reflections in the water and in the dull surfaces of metal mirrors, it was possible to find an image that corresponded accurately to what others saw. ... The use of the mirror signalled the beginning of introspective biography in the modern style: that is, not as a means of edification but as a picture of the self, its depths, its mysteries, its inner dimensions. ... The isolation of the world from the self – the method of the physical sciences – and the isolation of the self from the world – the method of introspective biography and romantic poetry – were complementary phases of a single process.

Self portraits of Rembrandt at the age of thirty-four and in the last year of his life, at sixty-three.

The mirror played an important part in the shift towards introspection and self-obsession. The epitome of this phenomenon was the use of the mirror in self-portraits. Perhaps the most memorable are the paintings by Rembrandt, who reassesses the essence of the ageing man he sees reflected in the glass. The flamboyant, youthful persona of his early self portraits

changes into a darker, more resigned character who is confronted with his own mortality.

The birth of individualism, the expansion of science and a new perception of the world: the thread that links these ideas, which represent the foundations of the Industrial Revolution in the West, is made of glass. Dr Samuel Johnson describes the miracle of this transparent material so many historians have overlooked:

Who when he first saw the sand and ashes by a casual intenseness of heat melted into a metalline form, rugged with excrescences and clouded with impurities, would have imagined that in this shapeless lump lay concealed so many conveniences of life as would, in time, constitute a great part of the happiness of the world. Yet by some such fortuitous liquifaction was mankind taught to procure a body at once in a high degree solid and transparent; which might admit the light of the sun, and exclude the violence of the wind; which might extend the sight of the philosopher to new ranges of existence, and charm him at one time with the unbounded extent of material creation, and at another with the endless subordination of animal life; and, what is of yet more importance, might supply the decays of nature, and succour old age with subsidiary sight. Thus was the first artificer in glass employed, though without his knowledge or expectation. He was facilitating and prolonging the enjoyment of life, enlarging the avenues of science, and conferring the highest and most lasting pleasures; he was enabling the student to contemplate nature, and the beauty to behold herself.

The final part of this chapter will follow the efforts of our historians to establish why glass-making and clock-making did not develop in the East, and to see if this might provide clues to the puzzle of why China did not industrialize before Europe.

In 1350 China was the most powerful nation on Earth. It had the most sophisticated culture, the largest trading fleet, the most efficient agriculture and a long history of inventive genius. Indeed, one theory is that because it was so far ahead, it paid little attention to what seemed trivial improvements in technology taking place in far-off lands away from the Middle Kingdom.

It is easy to fall into the trap of taking a Eurocentric view of China. The idea that China deliberately isolated itself from the West infuriates scholars of Chinese history. Christopher Cullen describes this view of China as being like the story of a headline in a British newspaper in the 1920s, before there was radar for channel crossings: 'FOG BLANKETS CHANNEL. CONTINENT ISOLATED.' As he puts it: 'The fact is that since the centre of the world economy was in the area of the Indian Ocean and East Asia for so long, the idea that it mattered remotely to China whether or not it had intimate connections with little foggy islands in north-western peninsulas is rather misleading.'

Nevertheless, the foggy islands went through some remarkable changes during the course of the next five centuries and it is interesting to try to pin down why the East evolved in such a different way. We have already looked at the contrasting attitudes to time measurement as a result of the development of the mechanical clock in Europe. The differences in glass production have an even greater impact.

By 1350 western Europe had three main uses for glass: windows, drinking vessels and jewellery. China used glass only for making cheap imitation jewellery. By 1600, when Europe was making mirrors and lenses, China had no significant glass-making capability. There was no shortage of skilled craftsmen and no reluctance to make things, particularly if they sold well. There was simply no demand.

China and Japan had no interest in glass windows. They used oiled paper to make beautiful opaque windows and screens. They glide elegantly on wooden runners and can be removed completely in the hot summer months. Japanese houses were constructed from bamboo and paper. The window frames could not support glass – which anyway, with the high frequency of earthquakes, would fall out and break. Glass production also uses large amounts of energy and resources. So why bother when there was a more appropriate paper alternative?

The national drink in China and Japan is hot tea. Wine glasses are ideally suited for cold red liquids, but not much use for hot green ones. Besides, China had porcelain – a product that the whole world wanted. Porcelain tea cups and bowls were luxuries the Chinese had developed to perfection. There was no place for glass in their society.

Traditional Japanese houses have sliding paper screens and windows called *shoji*.

By 1600, when the more important optical uses of glass were being exploited in the West, China and Japan had no tradition of glass- or clock-making, so the scientific developments associated with these technologies were less likely to happen in the East.

China and Japan remained largely oblivious to the rate of Western progress until European ships started to appear off the coast in the sixteenth century. Even then, from the Chinese point of view, the traders from the West had very little to offer except silver. The Europeans were eager to trade, to find new territory and expand their countries' empires. Christian missionaries began penetrating Asia and were met with increasing suspicion.

The Celestial Empire had good reason to be suspicious of the intentions of these foreign intruders, and rarely granted permission for travel inland. The only way to overcome these restrictions was to try to gain an audience with the emperor. One determined Italian missionary, Matteo Ricci, set off in 1602 with a collection of Western treasures that he hoped might secure his access to the Forbidden City. During the long journey north to Beijing, he delighted officials with demonstrations of his striking clocks and astrolabes. He wrote in his *Journal* in 1605: 'These globes, clocks, spheres, astrolabes, and so forth, which I have made and the use of which I teach, have gained me the reputation of being the greatest mathematician in the world. I do not have a single book on astronomy, but with only the help of certain ephemerides and Portuguese almanacs, I sometimes predict eclipses more accurately than they do.'

Eventually, after reaching the Forbidden City, he was disappointed to discover that he was not allowed inside the palace. He had to hand over the presents to the emperor's mandarins who were waiting outside the gates. Among the objects he presented were two mechanical clocks, two prisms, eight mirrors and a collection of bottles. He also had various Christian icons, including paintings of Christ and the Virgin Mary, a breviary and a cross inlaid with precious stones.

Matteo Ricci did not give up hope of meeting the emperor, and he waited in a local inn for news about how his gifts had been received. At first he was encouraged. The eunuchs reported that the emperor was infatuated with his mechanical clock and, more importantly for Ricci, when the Son of Heaven was shown the picture of the Son of God, he reacted with the words: 'This is a living idol.' However, the next report was less encouraging. The emperor had become afraid of this living God. Perhaps the Son of Heaven feared competition. Every day Ricci cross-examined the eunuchs in the hope of receiving a particular piece of news.

Before he gave the large clock to the emperor he wound up the mechanism with one last pull. He knew that within a couple of days it would stop. Sure enough, the clock ran down and stopped striking the

European alchemists often tried to mimic China's success in producing elegant porcelain, like this early fifteenth-century jar from the Ming Dynasty.

The Jesuit missionary Matteo Ricci (1552–1610) spent twenty-eight years in China. He learned to speak and write Chinese and was seen as 'the wise man from the West'.

hours. The emperor was furious and a messenger was dispatched to find Ricci and bring him to the palace. He became the first European to enter the Forbidden City. Once inside, he prolonged his stay in order to teach a group of eunuch mathematicians how to maintain the clock. They took meticulous notes and memorized every detail of the clock. They feared for their lives because the emperor was notoriously cruel. Many servants had been beaten to death for making some trivial mistake doing their duties.

When the clock was working, the emperor was happy again and Ricci's association with the palace continued. However, as David Landes points out: 'Ricci was fishing not merely for compliments but for souls. Implicit in this display of learning and technique was the argument that a civilization that could produce a manifestly superior science and technology must be superior in other respects, specifically in the spiritual realm. Clockwork was God's work.'

In the event, Ricci never actually got to meet the emperor, so his ambitious plan to convert him to Christianity failed. However, he did find out about the inner workings of the palace and introduced them to the mechanical workings of the clock. Subsequent emperors would collect mechanical clocks. They were seen as clever toys, but that is all they were – just entertaining gadgets of no consequence to be locked away in a vast hall. These were the emperor's machines and would not be widely available in China for centuries. Time still belonged to the emperor.

When the Jesuits brought mechanical clocks to Japan, there was a rather different reaction. The Japanese wanted to produce their own clocks, but thought the Western system of dividing the day into twenty-four equal hours did not reflect the true complexity of nature. Summer daylight hours should be long and winter ones short. In order to achieve this, Japanese clock-makers used two sets of spinning weights: one for day and one for night, which caused the clock to tick at different rates. Perhaps not surprisingly, these clocks were not very accurate and needed constant adjustment. These were precious objects for private display by the nobility, so clocks had very little impact on everyday life in Japan. The complex mechanism of the clocks showed that Japanese craftsmen had the intricate skills necessary, but they were skills for which there was little demand.

By the end of the sixteenth century, Christianity was spreading rapidly across China and Japan. Both countries' rulers began to resent the Jesuit infiltration. The missionaries and their newly converted followers became victims of a new policy of eradicating Western influence in China and Japan.

Christianity became so popular in Japan that the shoguns decided to banish missionaries. On a hill overlooking Nagasaki, twenty-six Christians were executed. In 1612 Christianity was officially banned and the churches destroyed. Over the next few decades the persecution intensified and this reinforced the passionate faith of Japanese Christians. In one of the worst incidents, they were rounded up and pushed off cliffs into boiling hot springs.

The shogunate wanted to shield Japan from Western influence, so it continued a series of measures in the 1630s that gradually cut off Japan from the rest of the world. First there was a ban on Japanese ships going overseas. Then Japanese citizens were not allowed to leave the country and those living abroad were not allowed to return. Foreign trade was banned and finally Europeans were not allowed to enter the country, thus completing Japan's isolation. Trade continued between China and Japan and other parts of Asia, but for the next two centuries the East was effectively closed to the West.

Foreigners were not allowed inside the Forbidden City until Matteo Ricci's clever ruse with the clock that stopped.

Detail from the memorial to the twenty-six Christian martyrs in Nagasaki.

Between 1650 and 1850 the exchange of ideas between the competing states of Europe was having a dramatic effect on the speed of change in the West. Japan had one tiny keyhole through which the achievements of the West could be glimpsed. It was the island of Dejima off the coast of Nagasaki. A small group of Dutch merchantmen were allowed to live on this island, provided they did not attempt to cross to mainland Japan.

The Japanese hoped to export ceramics, lacquerware and other highly decorated crafts, but the contact with the Dutch opened up other possibilities. A few privileged Japanese learned Dutch and found out about Western science and medicine. This vital link with the West would ultimately help Japan to modernize before China, as we will see in the next chapter.

Japanese craftsmen were famous for their fine workmanship, particularly for their intricate lacquer and woodblock prints. There was one invention from the West that would surely help prolong their working lives: spectacles. Yet very few glass lenses came to Japan during this period.

Alan Macfarlane was interested to find out why lens technology did not develop in the East until much later. He began to wonder whether it might have to do with differences in eyesight. While observing a group of Japanese students at Cambridge, he had noticed that even if they wore glasses they tended to read documents by bringing the print very close to their eyes. Their focusing problem was myopia rather than presbyopia.

He was curious to find out whether myopia was common in young people in Japan, so he visited Professor Tokoro, a leading eye doctor in Tokyo. He discovered that in primary schoolchildren around 30 per cent suffer from myopia. By secondary school it was over 50 per cent and by university almost 70 per cent. So the incidence was many times higher than in the West.

A similar pattern had been noticed in China by Otto Rasmussen, an American ophthalmic surgeon working in Shanghai in the 1920s. He thought it might explain why Chinese paintings had very sharply defined foregrounds and soft backgrounds with blurred mountains and clouds. He suggested three explanations for this high incidence of short sight. The first was a deficiency of vitamin A in the diet. He believed this was caused by a deterioration in the quality of food grown on over-cultivated and under-fertilized land. A second was genetic difference and the third explanation was connected to eye-strain. Reading and writing the fine detail of Chinese characters is very hard on the eyes. Add to that the interest in intricate crafts such as porcelain painting and lacquer work, rather than outdoor sports, and it is not hard to imagine that this could cause myopia. (Of course, it is also possible that the high incidence of myopia encouraged an interest in these activities.) Alan Macfarlane has another interesting theory: perhaps this obsession with miniature things had paved the way for their pre-eminence in micro-electronics and micro-engineering.

Clearly, then, there was a need for spectacles in the East – so why were they not produced in Japan? Professor Macfarlane believes there are several possible reasons. One factor is the age when people need glasses. In the West, as we have seen, the onset of presbyopia in middle-aged men could cut short their working lives by ten or twenty years. Just as they reached the height of their skills, they began to lose their sight, so there was a huge benefit if the length of their working lives could be doubled. In the East, the predominant optical problem was myopia, which affected young people before they were skilled. This handicap could be accommodated by simply peering more closely at objects, and it could also improve with age.

There was another technical obstacle. To correct myopia requires concave lenses, which are much harder to make than convex lenses. As the Japanese and Chinese had no tradition of making even simple convex lenses, it would be centuries before they were capable of making concave lenses.

Glass-making and clockwork are just two examples of technologies taken for granted in the West, but absent in the East. Although the hardware of these inventions is important, it is the underlying thought

The incidence of myopia is much higher among Japanese school children than Europeans. Could this help explain the Japanese interest in fine detail and their more recent success in micro-technology?

processes – the 'software' that created them – that really set them apart. The curious blend of competition, cooperation and collaboration encouraged a new way of thinking in the West. China had no competition from neighbouring states and little interest in the exchange of ideas. The Confucian, hierarchical political structure did nothing to encourage invention or individualism. There were plenty of entrepreneurs, but they were too far down the social ladder to have any impact on the economy. So for this brief chapter in the history of the world, it may appear that China was cruising along in the slow lane.

Although by this time technologically China may have been in limbo, economically it was still very much a force to be reckoned with.

The Great Exhibition of 1851 was the biggest show on Earth — a monument to the success of the Industrial Revolution.

The Chinese traded on a much grander scale than any of the European nations. However, as Joel Mokyr points out, things were about to change.

'By 1800, it may well have been true that trade with Europeans was a blip on the horizon, but you ignored them at your peril,' Professor Mokyr says. 'They would show up one day with gun boats, and they would try to take your land and they would try to force you into humiliating peace conditions, and they would chunk large pieces of your cities away and turn them into free trading areas like the British did with Hong Kong. So, maybe they were a blip on the horizon – but, boy, that blip grew quickly.'

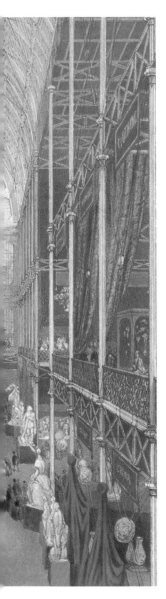

The supreme display of the triumph of the West was the Great Exhibition, which was housed in a cathedral of glass. It dominated the London skyline in 1851 and visitors flocked from all over the world to see this celebration of the Machine Age. Among them was the novelist Charlotte Brontë, who visited twice. Ironically, she compared the attractions of this public relations exercise for the West to an Eastern bazaar created by a genie.

It seems as if only magic could have gathered this mass of wealth from all the ends of the earth – as if none but supernatural hands could have arranged it thus, with such a blaze and contrast of colours and marvellous power of effect. The multitude filling the great aisles seems ruled and subdued by some invisible influence. Amongst the thirty thousand souls that people it the day I was there not one loud noise was to be heard, not one irregular movement seen; the living tide rolls on quietly, with a deep hum like the sea heard from the distance.

After it had been open for a month, the price of admission was reduced from a pound to a shilling. On the first 'shilling day' the masses came to view the eight miles of displays housed in this 'crystal palace' and unlike most of the gentry who came for the spectacle, the working people came to learn. The popularity of the industrial attractions was described in detail by Henry Mayhew in *1851*:

The machinery, which has been from the first the grand focus of attraction is on the 'shilling days', the most peculiar sight of the whole. Here every other man you rub against is habited in a corduroy jacket, or a blouse, or leathern gaiters; and round every object more wonderful than the rest, the people press, two and three deep, with their heads stretched out, watching intently the operations of the moving mechanism. You see the farmers, their dusty hats telling the distance they have come, with their mouths wide agape, leaning over the bars to see the self-acting mills at work, and smiling as they behold the frame spontaneously draw itself out, and then spontaneously run back again.

But the chief centres of curiosity are the power-looms, and in front of these are gathered small groups of artisans, and labourers, and young men whose red coarse hands tell you they do something for their living, all eagerly listening to the attendant as he explains the operations, after stopping the loom. ... At the steam brewery, crowds of men and women are continually ascending and descending the stairs; youths are watching the model carriages moving along the new pneumatic railway; indeed whether it be the noisy flax-crushing machine, or the splashing centrifugal pump, or the clatter of the Jacquard lace machine, or the bewildering whirling of the cylindrical steampress, – round each and all these are anxious, intelligent, and simple-minded artisans, and farmers, and servants, and youths, and children clustered, endeavouring to solve the mystery of its complex operations.

The fact is, the Great Exhibition is to them more of a school than a show. The working man has often little book-learning, but of such knowledge as constitutes the education of life – viz., the understanding of human motives, and the acquisition of power over natural forces, so as to render them subservient to human happiness – of such knowledge as this, we repeat, the working man has generally a greater share than those who are said to belong to the 'superior classes'. Hence it is, that what was a matter of tedium, and became ultimately a lounge for gentlefolks, is used as a place of instruction by the people.

For the engineers and inventors who had built the machines, there was a different kind of response. This was a showcase for the industrialized nations of the world and although Great Britain had enjoyed being the Mother of Invention for over half a century, there were the first signs that this was about to change. In the American pavilion was a dazzling display of ingenuity and invention. The farmers and artisans must have wondered how this upstart nation could have stolen the lead.

The frontier spirit and rapid expansion of this vast country had created a need for machines and tools that were easy to manufacture and simple to operate. America was in too much of a hurry for lengthy apprenticeships to enable new workers to learn how to operate complex machinery. The result was a collection of beautifully designed, easy-to-operate, elegant machines. Soon afterwards, Britain decided to dispatch a delegation of

engineers across the ocean to find out what was going on in the workshops of the New World.

Two hundred and fifty years after Matteo Ricci entered the Forbidden City, a Chinese junk sailed up the Thames. One of the sailors visited the Great Exhibition on the opening day. The sight of a Chinaman was so rare that after he bowed before Queen Victoria he was mistaken for an envoy and allowed to join the procession.

As he walked around afterwards, it is difficult to imagine what he thought as he surveyed this great glass showcase of Western achievement. He may have been unaware of his own country's scientific and technological traditions. Perhaps the Chinese sailor wondered why the most powerful nation on Earth seemed to have temporarily lost its lead. Queen Victoria may have sat on the throne of an Empire, but she was not the Daughter of Heaven. Looking around him at the businessmen, bankers and politicians, he might have noticed that this was a very different society. Not just more affluent, but more liberal, more free and more egalitarian. Here he could be master of his own time and space.

Yet the puzzle remains incomplete. Why was a European sailor not walking round a great hall of Eastern achievement? To widen the perspective, we will move back in time again, tracing a thousand years of history in the fields and battlefields of the East and West.

When Queen Victoria opened the Great Exhibition in Hyde Park, a Chinese sailor, who was mistaken for the ambassador, joined the VIPs at the opening ceremony.

Chapter Five

WAR AND PEACE

1,000 YEARS

Time: 900–1900
Place: Europe–Asia–
North America

The Commonwealth of Venice in their armoury have this inscription, 'Happy is that city which in time of peace thinks of war.'

ROBERT BURTON: THE ANATOMY OF MELANCHOLY (1621)

War and peace in three continents: the scope of this chapter is as ambitious as the Tolstoy novel from which it takes its title. Yet by looking at how these areas of human endeavour have differed between East and West, it is possible to find some important clues in the search for the origins of the Industrial Revolution.

Looking back over the past thousand years of history, it is easy to see war as a deadly aberration in mankind's peaceful progress towards a better world. Those who take a less moral view, however, might point to the unique opportunities that war offers for full employment, conspicuous consumption, mass production and technological development. Without war, some economic historians have argued, there would be no progress.

If this may seem to be an exceptionally cynical approach – which, of course, it is – it is one unfortunately borne out by the evidence of much of this chapter. War is competition at its fiercest, its demands on inventors

Planting rice in a paddy field: a laborious and back-breaking task.

more urgent than the market forces of the most cut-throat capitalist society. If a country opts out of the battle – as China did when it retreated into the shadow of its Great Wall – it may save generations of young men from senseless slaughter. However, it also runs the risk of finding itself in a technological backwater.

The military hardware that enabled the West to pulverize the rest of the world had a direct impact on domestic technology, as we will see. Arguably, without the cannon, the steam engine would never have been invented. At the same time, the peaceful pursuit of agriculture developed in widely differing ways in the West and East. The fundamental difference between them is obvious: one half of the world grows rice, the other grows hard grains. The bent-backed woman planting rice under a hot sun in a flooded paddy field; the placid oxen harnessed to the plough … both symbolize the divergent attitudes to human labour that were

Chinese workers preparing steel wire to be used in compasses. The Chinese had discovered how to make magnetized compass needles by the eleventh century — six centuries before the Europeans.

a critical factor in the creation of the modern world. While eastern Asia maintained hard, physical toil in an *industrious* revolution, western Europe embarked on a course that would replace human labour with machines – an *industrial* revolution.

Agriculture and warfare are both activities that demand tremendous exertion of energy and tie up significant parts of the working population. Both benefit enormously from advances in efficiency, however chilling a concept this may sound when applied to the business of killing people. The first country to make the leap from hand-to-hand fighting to devastation at a distance wins the war; the farmer with the most efficient machines avoids famine. Less tangibly, efficiency frees people from daily drudgery, leaving them the mental energy for other things we have come to consider essential.

An economic forecaster looking down on the planet in AD900 could well have picked China as the civilization destined for early success. It has been estimated that possibly more than half of the basic inventions and discoveries upon which the modern world depends originated in China. Not only paper (and paper money), printing and gunpowder, but also the compass (which originally had its needle pointing south rather than north), the stirrup and the humble wheelbarrow. When Lady Mary Wortley Montagu told her English friends about her 'discovery' of smallpox inoculation in Turkey in the eighteenth century (as we saw in Chapter Three), she was merely passing on a technique that had been known in China for 800 years.

So, given all that technological fertility, the natural and often-asked question is: why was China not the place where the Industrial Revolution happened? Our historian Christopher Cullen says, 'Efforts have been made to answer that question by trying to find factors which in some way inhibited or stopped China having an industrial revolution, but I think scholars today would very largely want to deny that it is a legitimate question at all. It's like asking why there are no unicorns nowadays. There just aren't any unicorns ... the Industrial Revolution did not happen in China.

'It's quite clear that having an industrial revolution is not about having some kind of special mechanical genius in your nation for being techno-logically inventive, because the Chinese had had plenty of that. It must perhaps depend on some rather specific things that happened in particular times and particular places in a very chancy way.'

Alan Macfarlane's search for an answer to the riddle has led him to become interested in the comparative anthropology of two very different countries: Japan and Nepal. Although now a modern industrialized nation, Japan had its industrial revolution relatively late, having spent much of its history in the shadow of China. The people of Nepal, by contrast, still live a way of life that has changed little over the past thousand years.

We will look at Japan's rapid transformation – from a feudal state ruled by shoguns and samurai to one of the most important industrial powers on Earth – later in the chapter. For the moment, our focus is on rural Nepal, where adult life still revolves around the back-breaking demands of work in the fields, without the aid of complex tools or machines.

Alan Macfarlane first visited Nepal in 1968, working for fifteen months as an anthropologist among a people called the Gurungs. Since then, he has made many extended visits to the Himalayan village of Thak, building up a uniquely detailed study of this remote settlement. He and his wife, Sarah Harrison, now have their own house in the village, and have been 'adopted' by one of the families. This adoption is not simply a polite gesture to a foreigner; it is a bond deeply felt on both sides. When Alan Macfarlane's 'sister' Dilmaya died at the early age of forty-two, he aban-doned his final lecture in Cambridge to go and perform the duties of a brother in her memorial ritual.

For him, part of Nepal's fascination is that it is one of the few places left in the world where it is possible to experience what daily life must have been like before the Industrial Revolution. As he puts it in the introduction to *The Savage Wars of Peace*: 'Witnessing the perennial problem of disease, the sanitary arrangements, the illness of young children, the difficulties with water, the flies and worms, the gruelling

Alan Macfarlane and Sarah Harrison with their adopted Nepalese family. The marigold garlands are a traditional symbol of friendship and hospitality.

work and the struggle against nature in a mountain community made clear to me, in a way that books or even films alone could never do, some of the realities which the English and Japanese faced historically.'

The isolation of Thak is obviously the most important reason why so little has changed. The people are prisoners of their habitat. The only way of living a modern life is to leave the village, and increasingly that is what many young people do. Those who are left face an arduous struggle for existence based on hard physical labour.

'Because of the terrain, you can't have the penetration of all the technologies of modern civilization,' says Alan Macfarlane. 'You can't have cars, you don't have electricity, you don't have mains water, you don't have mains sanitation. So, when you come here you're moving back at least a thousand years in history, and you're seeing what it must have been like over most of the world before all these things happened. So you see people using their bodies, their backs, their legs, their arms, and also animals and plants to wrest a living from this terribly rugged terrain.'

Even the humble wheelbarrow is nowhere to be seen. This was an invention known to the Chinese as early as the first century BC but, in much of Asia, the human back was the preferred system of transport. Wheels existed in Asian culture – the Buddhist prayer wheel is an example – but they were not seen as being of much practical use. Looking at the lack of roads, and the narrow paths along the rice terraces, it is easy to see why. Alan Macfarlane quotes the example of the British officer in India, who was horrified to see people carrying stones on their heads. He tried to 'civilize' the natives by giving them wheelbarrows. The next day he found them marching along with the wheelbarrows on their heads – and the stones inside.

The villagers of Thak grow rice in the lower half of the valley, and the hard grains of Europe higher up the mountainside – another reason the settlement fascinates Alan Macfarlane. For it is the different demands of these two crops that he sees as an important key to the differing development of East and West.

'Rice produces far more grain per head than the hard grains of Europe, and that allows you to have much higher densities of population, so Asia became heavily populated while Europe was lightly populated,' he says.

'Secondly, each plant can be carefully grown like a vegetable. With hard grains like wheat, you just grow a field of them and it doesn't make much advantage if you tend each little plant very carefully, and water and weed it. So there's no advantage of having more labour and applying it. Wet rice is very labour-intensive. Each plant has to be planted singly. You have to keep weeding it, and cutting it is difficult. So it does require dense populations, whereas dry grains don't.'

The remote settlement of Thak, where villagers grow whatever they can in difficult and mountainous terrain.

Sturdy but slow: a pair of oxen represent the first stage in the enslavement of animals.

While it is growing, rice is a crop that absorbs human labour almost as it absorbs water during cooking. However, once the crop is successfully harvested, the rest is relatively easy. It is simply a question of removing the outer husk from the rice, boiling it, then eating it. So, for much of east Asia – apart from the wheat belt in northern China – agriculture revolved around this relatively simple crop. There was plenty of available manual labour, and no real incentive to mechanize. Even the use of domestic animals largely disappeared.

Europe had no slaves or coolies and a climate that was unsuitable for rice. What is more, the hard grains favoured by European farmers required an extra stage to make them palatable: grinding, or milling. The land had to be cleared of forest, the heavy soil tilled, the grains harvested and the wheat ground into flour. So Europeans devised ways of supplementing their labour. From oxen, they moved on to horses harnessed to metal ploughs with wheels; they forged iron agricultural tools and used water wheels and windmills.

Alan Macfarlane's study of work patterns across the globe has led him to uncover an uncomfortable truth about the West: we are lazy. Instead of using human slaves to save our own backs, we enslaved animals. The Chinese had invented horse harnesses, but never used them on a wide scale. Europeans took up the invention, adding blinkers to keep the horse's mind on the job, and metal shoes – producing, as Alan Macfarlane puts it, a 'metal and animal machine'.

Horses had the great advantage over oxen of being able to move quickly over long distances, making it possible for people to live quite far away from their farms. At the same time, the agricultural revolution led to a significant decline in the number of people working on the land, and a massive growth in the urban population. In the East, by contrast, large numbers of people needed to remain in the countryside to help work the fields.

Quite apart from the practical consequences of using animals, the technology involved was a vital factor in the Industrial Revolution. The farrier, the blacksmith, the wheelwright and the woodman ... these craftsmen were responsible for the first steps towards industrialization. A skilled farrier can make the process of shoeing a horse look simple; in reality, it is a piece of precision engineering. A slight miscalculation, and the horse would be hurt just as a human would be if nail scissors cut into the quick of a nail.

Similarly, the windmills and watermills that continued the process of harnessing nature used carefully balanced cogs and wheels. These have been linked to clock-making technology, which – as we saw in the previous chapter – was an important precursor to industrialization. In 1086, the Domesday Book listed 5,624 watermills for some 3,000 communities, which meant an average of perhaps two mills for every village. By this time, the mill had two main uses: for grinding grains to produce flour for bread, and for cleaning, or fulling, cloth. (In the latter case, heavy wooden

Horses ploughing in a typical British landscape: 'metal and animal machines' supported by a team of skilled craftsmen.

hammers lifted and dropped by the water wheel replaced the trampling feet of the fullers.) In the twelfth century, these watermills were joined by the more complicated windmills.

'In order to maintain these mills, to build them in the first place, and then to keep them working, you'd need a whole lot of proto-engineers, people who understood how machinery works, who could repair it, could build it, who could think of ways of improving it,' says Alan Macfarlane. 'So you get, from a thousand years ago, a civilization beginning to emerge which is based on engineering, on the use of non-human power, and thinking carefully about how to transform this.

'So what we think of as the Industrial Revolution of the eighteenth century is really the final effect of something which started hundreds of years earlier, and has led to people thinking deeply about how you can use natural force to help human beings survive in a difficult environment.'

Among the early users of watermills were Benedictine monks – as we saw in the previous chapter, their order readily exploited labour-saving gadgets. This approach was encouraged by their founder: the *Rule of St Benedict* stated that: 'The monastery ought if possible to be so constituted that all things necessary, such as water, a mill, a garden, and the various crafts might be contained within it.'

Generally, however, only rich landowners could afford the capital outlay required to build mills. In most villages, that rich landowner would be the lord of the manor, who would provide the wood from his estate, and probably also the labour to build a new mill. In return, he would expect all the villagers to use it – even if they had their own rotary querns. In some places, hand querns were banned, or even smashed. The lord of the manor would thus enjoy a monopoly, and this helped to strengthen the emerging feudal system. It also, of course, foreshadowed the development of capitalism.

As Alan Macfarlane says, 'It's no accident that the first great industrial steam-powered buildings were called mills.' The first factories of the Industrial Revolution operated on the same principle: creating a monopoly, centralizing production and investing large amounts of money in labour-saving machinery. Richard Arkwright, who as we saw in Chapter Two ruthlessly insisted on selling his cotton-spinning machines in batches of a thousand, may have been of a different social class from those early lords of the manor. However, he was still operating on the same principle – enforcing a monopoly in order to make profit for himself.

So why did mills not develop on the same scale in the East? We already know that the answer does not appear to lie in lack of technical expertise. The Chinese were using water-powered bellows for blast furnaces, and chain pumps that could raise water by as much as 15 feet, as early as the first century AD. (The first European chain pumps, modelled directly on Chinese designs, were not made until the sixteenth century.) Christopher

Cullen points out that during the great age of Chinese monasticism, from AD600 to 900, Buddhist monasteries had so many water wheels that people complained they were clogging up the waterways. 'So there's no sense that using mechanical power from water is something the Chinese were not interested in.'

Part of the explanation seems to be that by the Middle Ages, the Chinese simply had no need of mills. Theirs was predominantly a rice culture, which meant that there was no need to grind grain. Their paper was made from the mulberry bush rather than rags, so there was no need for pulping mills; and as they used primarily cotton and hemp, they had no need for fulling mills to clean wool fleeces either. This lack of milling meant that the improvements in gearing and machine-making, which would continue in the West, passed the East by.

One of the mysteries of Chinese history is the way the Chinese people themselves appeared to develop a collective amnesia about their own very considerable technological achievements. It is only in the past few decades, with the efforts of scholars inspired by Joseph Needham, author of the monumental fifteen-volume *Science and Civilization in China*, that the balance is being redressed. As Deputy Director of the Needham Institute in Cambridge, Christopher Cullen is very much part of this movement.

Two main reasons seem to emerge for the technological vacuum that developed in China: its social structure, and its isolation. For much of its history – as we saw in the previous chapter – China regarded itself as the centre of the world: the Middle Kingdom. The eighteenth-century French Jesuit missionary P. J. B. Du Halde wrote:

There is no Nation more proud of their pretended Grandeur, and their assumed Preheminence over all others. This Haughtiness, which is born with them, inspires even the Rabble with the greatest Contempt for all other Nations. They are so full of their own Country, Customs, Manners, and Maxims, that they cannot be persuaded there is any Thing good out of China, or any Truth but what their learned Men are acquainted with. However, they have seen their Mistake a little, since the Europeans came among them; tho', when they first saw them, they asked if they had any Cities, Towns, or Houses in Europe.

Du Halde's view may, of course, have been coloured by frustration at the apparent imperviousness of the Chinese soul to his Christian message. However, as Christopher Cullen points out, if they did give off an air of superiority to outsiders, it was not without good reason.

'China was producing commodities that the outside world desired a great deal, like fine porcelain, silk and tea,' he says. 'People were prepared to sail thousands of miles to buy this stuff and to pay for it in hard cash. They had to pay for it in hard cash, because there wasn't anything that the Chinese wanted to buy, particularly the Chinese in south China, who were not interested in buying nice solid English woollen cloth to keep them warm in their Cantonese weather.

'So there were plenty of people coming to get things from China, but China was not in the business of sailing long distances to take these things abroad.'

This attitude was reinforced by government legislation that made it illegal for Chinese shipbuilders to construct a sea-going boat with more than two masts.

'In the fifteenth century, China had achieved immense triumphs in penetrating the outside world with seaborne expeditions going away as far as Africa, but why the political decision was taken in the Ming court to cut that activity off so quickly after the 1430s is still something of a mystery,' says Christopher Cullen. 'It seems to have been that some of the conservative circles at court decided that this was a distraction from the primary activity of the State, which should be to support agriculture, that all this sailing abroad and gadding about was just a waste of time.

'There was also something else about the Chinese government at this time. It was structured in a way which tried, with a very small government machine, to keep control of a huge country. Anything that went out of the zone of control, anything that got too big or too complicated for the government to keep its hands on, was a threat.'

A modern reconstruction of would-be mandarins taking the Chinese civil service exams.

Du Halde wrote at some length about the domination of the emperor in a system of government he described as more despotic than any monarchy. 'The emperor is vested with absolute Authority, and to appearance is a kind of Divinity; the Respect which is paid him amounting to a sort of Adoration. His Words are like so many Oracles, and the least of his Commands as implicitly obey'd as if they came down from Heaven. None are suffer'd to speak to him but on their Knees, not even his eldest brother; or to appear before him with Ceremony in any other Posture, unless he gives Orders to the contrary.'

In the early days of the emperors, China's celebrated imperial bureaucracy had fostered some ambitious projects. However, it had increasingly became a force for conservatism. Those hoping to join the élite mandarin ruling class had to submit themselves to a fearsome examination process, which involved sitting in a tiny cell for an average of five days. They were expected to be able to quote accurately from Confucian classics – and several measures were taken to exclude the possibility of cheating or bribery. The question to be answered by each examinee was decided only at the last moment by firing an arrow at a list. Each student was given a number and each script was copied out by a scribe, so students could not be identified by their calligraphy.

The principle of the selection procedure was meritocratic. However, a whole series of exams was required to get to the top, and preparation for the first one alone took an average of six years. This made the whole process impractical for a peasant's son without a wealthy sponsor, or a tradition of office-holding in the family. Similarly, under the Ming dynasty, rote learning and strict orthodoxy became essential for success. Essays had to be written according to a set form, with a specified number of sections, linked in specified ways, sometimes even using a set number of characters. This, coupled with the fact that the examiners were themselves products of the system, created an atmosphere of conformity.

'The stress of taking the official's examination was certainly very high indeed,' says Christopher Cullen. 'You were expected, if you were presented with a mere fragment of one of the texts you were supposed to have studied, to recollect whole chunks of it. However, it also tested intelligence and ability to think fast under stress. Although it seems to us a very artificial test, it was very effective in finding people who were highly determined, highly intelligent and could think straight when they knew that a lot depended on it. It was probably a good way of selecting a generalist official.

'We mustn't forget that in Britain, too, in the nineteenth century, when Civil Service examinations were first adopted in place of selling jobs, one way that you could get a job, say in the high Civil Service, was to demonstrate your skill in composing Greek verse. The sort of people who went in for these examinations, having had a public school education, a university education, may well have studied the ancient Western classics in the same way that their Chinese colleagues would have studied the ancient Chinese classics. So it isn't too strikingly different, really.'

Apart from the emperor, the real governing power in China was exercised by the scholar official class, recruited through these examinations. Only a tiny minority were ever presented at court. However, undaunted by the high failure rate, many young hopefuls continued to take and re-take the exams, in the hope of bettering their family's prospects. China had no hereditary nobility with political power, and gentry status was assured for those who succeeded in the lower degree-level examinations. The qualification gave family members exemption from corporal punishment, and access not only to the local magistrate but to a whole network of connections that were essential for both social and economic survival.

The nineteenth-century political writer and thinker Alexis de Tocqueville was extremely scornful of this aspect of Chinese society. As he put it in the second volume of *Democracy in America*, published in 1840: 'There is no need for me to say that this universal and uncontrolled desire for official appointments is a great social evil, that it undermines every citizen's sense of independence and spreads a venal and servile temper throughout the nation.'

De Tocqueville was convinced that it was China's bureaucracy that had stifled innovation and originality. As he put it: 'The Chinese, following in their fathers' steps, had forgotten the reasons which guided them. They still used the formula without asking why. They kept the tool but had no skill to adapt or replace it. ... They had to copy their ancestors the whole time in everything for fear of straying into impenetrable darkness if they deviated for a moment from their tracks.'

This, coupled with the all-pervasive power of the emperor, could partly explain why China did not have an equivalent of the European scientific revolution. If the emperor was interested in a particular aspect of scientific investigation, progress would be made. If he was not interested, it would not. In Europe, if your ideas did not take off in one country, you could try another. In China there was nowhere else to go.

The all-powerful emperor: an eighteenth-century painting showing the Chinese emperor turning the first sod of earth of the agricultural year.

However, Christopher Cullen is cautious about such easy explanations. As he puts it: 'I think it would be too simple to say that China was not as inventive, say, as late-eighteenth-century and early-nineteenth-century Britain simply because it had an imperial system, and a highly centralized government. Otherwise how would you explain the fact that China was so inventive earlier on, when it still had the same system of imperial government and the civil service?

'We must look to other factors, and I think perhaps we have to look to the particular circumstances of eighteenth- and nineteenth-century Britain, and what happened there, in ways that would have been very difficult to reproduce in China because of the different social circumstances.'

One crucial difference was the absence in China of the powerful urban merchant classes, the bourgeoisie, who sponsored many of the innovations in Europe.

'The Chinese bureaucracy was small, but highly effective,' says Christopher Cullen. 'Through the network that started with the county magistrate at the bottom and went all the way up to high ministers of State and the emperor at the top, a system of knowledge going up and orders coming down was imposed over the whole country.

'There was no alternative source of political power permitted. There was nothing in China equivalent to, say, the corporation of the City of London. There was no municipal power, apart from the emperor's power. Every city was the emperor's city, and the concept of being a citizen of a city was completely lacking. This meant that in China there was not a chance of the urban merchant classes coming to anything like the position of decisive influence that they came to have in many European countries.'

An example is the way merchants in the City of London were prepared to put money into improvements in navigation and ship design.

'They knew that it was vital to their business development that these things should advance. In China, on the other hand, it would have been regarded as a very suspicious act if a bunch of merchants had got together to fund ways of building ships to go far overseas, when the emperor had already made himself quite plain that he didn't really want this to happen.'

Merchants had a social status well below that of the scholar gentry, and their only hope of finding a voice in political affairs was for a member of their family to pass the necessary examinations.

'As merchants, their job was to engage in business and to pay their taxes, and they could be subject to a huge amount of arbitrary official power, amounting effectively to random confiscations of their wealth,' says Christopher Cullen. 'The Chinese government had always been concerned that there would be some alternative centre of political power developed, and we have to remember that its task was quite a considerable one, keeping the country governed with a really very small number of people.

'So the process of penalizing merchants from time to time if they looked too rich and independent was one that Chinese governments followed certainly for 2,000 years, and continued to follow quite successfully up to the present century.'

Clearly then, social conditions in China meant that it was in the interests of the ruling class to maintain the status quo. There was limited scope for the individual entrepreneur, and little incentive to move towards industrialization in a country where there were plenty of pairs of hands to do the work. However, it was a long time before either the Chinese or the Europeans realized just how differently things were evolving in East and West.

'Adam Smith, writing in the second half of the eighteenth century, was still saying that China was the world's richest country, and the one long renowned for pre-eminence in agriculture,' says Christopher Cullen. 'I would not say that it was until any earlier than 1800 that the point came where it was quite clear that Westerners were doing things that the Chinese would have done well to take notice of. Though whether or not having, say, a Boulton and Watt steam engine set up to pump water in some agriculture reclamation scheme rather than using more traditional Chinese water-raising methods would have really enabled anyone to make more money in China, I can't say.'

This brings us to another element in the picture: the history of technological development. In many ways, this was determined by the nature of the materials available. In the East, craftsmen became masters in the use of soft materials like paper, wood, and bamboo. To this day, scaffolding on buildings in China is made from bamboo, rather than metal.

Bamboo is actually a grass – though it can grow as tall as a tree – and has many uses. 'Westerners find it very difficult to realize how important bamboo was, and is, in Japan and China,' says Alan Macfarlane. 'It grows very easily, it propagates easily, it can be easily cut, easily shaped, it's very strong, you can bend it into any shape, you don't need to make joints, you can tie it with rope and string. Anyone can work it – you don't need occupational specialization. So you get a whole civilization that is based on bamboo. This means that you don't have any need for iron, you don't have any need for stone for buildings, you don't have any need for wood turners and woodworkers. So Europe went towards wood, stone and iron, and Japan and China went towards this wonderful substance, bamboo.'

This was a short cut that gave China and Japan a great advantage – but also, in some ways, led to a dead end. Over the centuries, craftsmen produced more and more intricate and beautiful objects. Bamboo was lashed into frames and walls for houses, and carved into tools. However, it was not possible to make wheels or cogs or axles from bamboo, so the East lost out on craft skills that formed a vital precursor to technological development.

Japanese Samurai armour. The silk cords which were used to attach various parts could have symbolic meanings; flame and gold cords, for example, originally denoted a princely family.

The Industrial Revolution in the West started with wood and water, then moved on to coal and iron. However, that is not to say that coal and iron were unknown in the East – far from it. Du Halde reported in the eighteenth century that China had untold treasures lying beneath its mountains, but that there were political obstacles to mining, particularly precious metals.

'The Mountains of China are still more valuable, on account of the Mines of different Metals. The Chinese say they are full of Gold and Silver; but that the working of them hitherto has been hindered from some political Views, perhaps, that the publick Tranquillity might not be disturbed by the too great abundance of these Metals, which would make the People haughty and negligent of Agriculture.'

China had coal and iron mines – and, in fact, used coal-fired blast furnaces to produce cast iron as early as the fourth century BC. It was at first the preserve of private speculators, who grew rich from it. But the Han Dynasty nationalized all cast-iron manufacture in 119 BC so that the emperor could monopolize it. As in Europe, there were iron agricultural tools, pots and pans. However, the most visible uses of iron were in the large showpieces, such as the 20-foot-high Great Lion of Tsang-chou in Hopei Province, erected in the year 954 by Emperor Shih Tsung.

In medieval Europe, the blacksmith would have been one of the most important people in a village. In China and Japan, however, there was no equivalent, as iron was so little used in everyday life. There were no horses to be shoed and, while metal was used in agricultural tools, it was often only for the tips. Metal remained scarce until well into the nineteenth century. The great Japanese modernizer, Yukichi Fukuzawa (to whom we will return later in this chapter), was to notice this above all else when he joined the first Japanese mission to the United States in 1860. As he wrote in his autobiography: 'There seemed to be an enormous waste of iron everywhere. In garbage piles, on the sea-shores – everywhere – I found lying old oil cans, empty cans, and broken tools. This was remarkable to us, for in Yedo [the old name for Tokyo] after a fire, there would appear a swarm of people looking for nails in the ashes.'

It is no coincidence that when the eighteenth-century economist Adam Smith was looking for an example to illustrate what he saw as the central essence of the modern world, he chose a nail factory. Growing up in Scotland, he had witnessed at first hand how the principle of division of labour had greatly increased the dexterity and efficiency of a team of workers.

A common smith, who, though accustomed to handle the hammer, has never been used to make nails, if upon some particular occasion he is obliged to attempt it, will scarce, I am assured, be able to make above two or three hundred nails in a day, and those too very bad ones. A smith who has been accustomed to make nails, but whose sole or principal business has not been that of a nailer, can seldom with his utmost diligence make more than eight hundred or a thousand nails in a day. I have seen several boys under twenty years of age who had never exercised any other trade but that of making nails, and who, when they exerted themselves, could make, each of them, upwards of two thousand three hundred nails in a day.

In the East, the major use of metal was weapons. Perhaps the best-known example in Japan was the samurai sword, the making of which became elevated to a high art form. Here, the emphasis was on craftsmanship rather than manufacturing efficiency. The sword had great spiritual significance for its bearer – even the process of forging and making the blade originally required religious observances. The endless heating, beating and re-shaping of different grades of steel, and hours and hours of fine polishing, produced a weapon of unique flexibility and legendary sharpness. Each blade would be months in the making, and when finished would be carefully inscribed with the crafts-man's name and the date.

A samurai sword was not only an exquisitely crafted deadly weapon, it was also the symbol of office for the samurai class, who were the élite civil servants and warriors of the emperor. The blade of a sword might well be handed down from father to son and be rehilted when necessary for differ-ent purposes. As recently as the Second World War, it was not unknown for Japanese officers to carry family swords that dated back 400 or 500 years. The craft continued long after the sword had any value as a weapon. Its shape and length varied over the centuries, but changes in design had little impact on the sword's function.

A typically ferocious Samurai warrior, the traditional pair of swords — one short, one long — at his belt.

The Japanese were also great archers, using longbows made of strips of seasoned bamboo and other woods. These were lacquered, and bound together with vegetable glues and fibres. They had a proud tradition of meticulously crafted and elaborate armour, which used metal as well as leather and various other fabrics. This required hours of labour in applying the many coats of lacquer that produced its distinctive shiny finish.

In the history of Japanese military technology, there had been a steady improvement up until the thirteenth century, when they twice repelled invasions by the Chinese. The Chinese had a number of weapons that the Japanese would have done well to copy, including crossbows and rockets using gunpowder. The crossbow had the great advantage over the longbow that it required no special strength, and was as easy to use as a modern handgun. Gunpowder, as we know, was the key to the future evolution of weaponry, so the Japanese resisted this innovation at their peril. However, for the time being, they stuck to traditional weapons. They felt secure in their island status and, since the following three centuries were dominated by civil, rather than foreign wars, there was little incentive to change.

'Within Japan, it was very uniform and very well controlled – so basic-ally warfare was like a game,' says Alan Macfarlane. 'It was different clans fighting each other with the traditional weapons. If you're playing cricket against friends you don't suddenly change the cricket bat into some other kind of implement that is better, because everyone knows what the rules are and you continue with the same tools.

'In Europe you had all these different competing military regimes very close together, so if the Spanish or the Italians suddenly invented a new weapon, then you had to adopt it, otherwise you would be destroyed. So when, for example, gunpowder weapons were developed in Europe, within twenty or thirty years they were being used very widely. So it was the strong, aggressive military conflicts of Europe that led to the very rapid evolution of weapons in Europe. Whereas in Japan it was a peaceful place in some ways, it was just local sport.'

Firearms were first introduced into Japan by some Portuguese castaways in the mid sixteenth century, and they were quickly copied by Japanese metalsmiths. Guns were largely instrumental in reunifying Japan during a period of civil war – but once this task had been completed, they were banned. Foreign imports of all kinds – including Christianity, at this time – were distrusted, and there were worries that guns might have a destabilizing effect on society.

'This is perhaps the only time in history that I know of when a great civilization has decided to go backwards, and banned weapons,' says Alan Macfarlane. 'It is an extraordinary thing, and it is also encouraging because it shows that we could get rid of weapons, if we really wanted to, in this modern world.'

At the same time as the ban on firearms, a series of sword hunts were carried out, aimed at removing weapons from all except the privileged samurai class. Some of the confiscated swords were melted down to make a great metal Buddha at Kyoto, while others were kept in State arsenals for use in emergencies. Following this, there was a period of splendid isolation known in Japanese history as the 'great peace', which lasted for 250 years. This brought its own rewards – but inevitably meant that military skill declined. The samurai retainers with their outdated armour and swords were to be no match for the Europeans when they came back in the nineteenth century with up-to-date weapons. And by missing out on the precision engineering that went with the military technology, the Japanese were left behind in more than the arms race.

Meanwhile, what had happened to the Chinese, who had come up with the invention of gunpowder in the first place? In many ways, their story parallels that of the Japanese – except, of course, that many of the developments that were to give the Europeans the military lead had originated in China.

The Invention of Gunpowder and the First Casting of Bronze Cannon, from an early seventeenth-century European engraving. Gunpowder had been known to the Chinese centuries earlier.

The Venice Arsenal: a city within a city, with production-line efficiency. The crenellated sixteenth-century towers suggest the area's military purpose, while the lion on the left of the picture is a war trophy.

The great irony of gunpowder was that it was invented not by people looking for better weapons, but by Chinese alchemists seeking the elixir of immortality. A crucial ingredient was saltpetre, or potassium nitrate, which generally forms natural deposits only in hot climates and was relatively rare in Europe. In 1067, the year after William the Conqueror won the Battle of Hastings (with bows and arrows), the Chinese emperor had been so concerned about the dangers of gunpowder that he banned the sale of saltpetre and sulphur to foreigners.

Gunpowder apart, a horrifying barrage of weapons was available to the Chinese from very early on. Smoke bombs, poison and tear gas from the fourth century BC; flares, bombs, grenades and mines from the tenth century AD. Perhaps most relevant to the current discussion, however, is the early development of the industrialization of warfare in China. The standard weapon of the Chinese soldier was the crossbow – and, from inscriptions on surviving examples, it is clear that each different part of the bow was made by different people, showing an early use of division of labour. Weapons manufacture was centrally controlled and, by 1160, the annual output of the imperial armaments office had reached over three million weapons a year.

In the West, the only place to produce armaments on such an industrial scale at this time was Venice. The Venice Arsenal, founded in 1104, and enlarged in the fourteenth to sixteenth centuries, so impressed foreigners by its size and efficiency that 'arsenal' came into the language as a general term for a place to manufacture and store weapons. The word derives from the Arabic, *darsina'a*, meaning 'house of industry' – and this is exactly what it was. The great Italian poet Dante took inspiration for part of his *Inferno* from the dark vats of boiling tar, and scenes of hellish military efficiency that he saw there.

At its busiest, the Arsenal was manned by a workforce of up to 16,000 *arsenalotti*, a highly skilled team of master shipbuilders. It was a self-contained industrial city dedicated to building and refitting fighting ships. The ship parts were mass-produced and interchangeable, and the entire complex was laid out like a floating conveyer belt. Using an assembly line system, the vessels were towed past a succession of windows to collect ropes, sails, armaments – even ship's biscuits.

By the late sixteenth century, when Venice was faced with the threat posed by the ever-stronger Ottoman Empire, the Arsenal reached a peak of efficiency. This was demonstrated to the young Henri III of France, who visited Venice in 1574. He was taken to the Arsenal one morning to see the keel of a ship being laid – then was invited back after a feast that evening to see the launching of the same ship, fully equipped and ready for the open sea.

Visitors to the Arsenal today can still see the high crenellated walls and impressive gateway, flanked by stone lions looted from Piraeus, near Athens. However, there are few other visible remains of the scene of industry that once lay behind this grand façade. Like so much else in Venice, it is simply a reminder of past glories. As Ruskin put it, in *The Stones of Venice* (1853), much of the city is: 'a ghost upon the sands of the sea, so weak – so quiet – so bereft of all but her loveliness, that we might well doubt, as we watched her faint reflection in the mirage of the lagoon, which was the City, and which the Shadow'.

Canaletto's painting of Ascension Day celebrations in Venice shows the Republic in its full glory. In the centre, the scarlet-and-gold state barge is waiting to take the Doge across the Lagoon for a ceremony that symbolized Venetian domination of the seas.

Venice, once the strongest maritime power on Earth, went into decline once trade routes to America and the East started to open up. The balance of maritime power shifted to the European ports with access to America, such as Amsterdam, Lisbon and London. Militarily, despite their spectacular defeat of the Turks in the Battle of Lepanto in 1571, the Venetians were outgunned. At Lepanto, the Turks lost 200 galleys, together with their artillery, stores and some 30,000 men – yet, within seven months, they had replaced all their losses and were again able to send a major battle fleet to the West. What is worse, they had imitated the Venetians' 'secret weapon' – the galeass, which looked like a merchant supply ship but was in fact a heavily armed warship.

The Venetians thus became a victim of their own success – a story that was endlessly repeated throughout the long and bloody history of European warfare. In an atmosphere of constant competition, everyone was perpetually on the lookout for new ideas. They came, they saw – and they copied.

Like the Venetians, the Chinese were well placed for the industrial production of armaments. Guns had appeared in China by the thirteenth century, and cast-iron cannons were produced before Europeans had even learned how to make cast iron. One of the myths of history is that the Chinese were such a peaceable people that they were only really interested in using their invention of gunpowder for fireworks. This is simply not true. From early on, they had the capacity to produce large quantities of weapons, and demonstrated a willingness to use them.

However, like the Japanese, they missed out on a crucial stage in the evolution of gun and cannon design because their country was too peaceful. From 1300 to 1800, constant conflict in Europe led to dramatic advances in the loading, accuracy and range of weapons that changed the rules of engagement. Meanwhile, Japan was to some extent protected by its island status – but how did China manage to remain aloof?

The most visible symbol of the way China was increasingly turning her back on the rest of the world was the strengthening of the Great Wall during the Ming period (1368–1644). However, in reality, the wall offered only limited protection. It may have helped to keep out poorly armed barbarians by land, but it did nothing to protect China's vulnerable sea coast. Here, far from strengthening their sea defences, the Chinese appeared to be in retreat. Ambitious seagoing expeditions stopped, the navy was cut back, and its sailors ordered to sail inland, on the waters of the Grand Canal. Western ships were allowed to trade only in certain areas, and only if they temporarily removed their guns while in port.

Like the ostrich that puts its head in the sand, China was to pay dearly for its disregard of the military capabilities of foreigners. The Chinese junks, with their very high castles and no portholes for guns in the hull, were fit only for the traditional ramming and boarding sea battles. They were no match for the heavy guns of the West – as the Chinese discovered to their cost in the so-called Opium Wars of 1839–42.

These wars were the explosive result of a developing friction over trade between Britain and China. Official attempts through diplomatic channels to establish greater freedom of trade had been met with, at best, polite indifference. However, although the emperor made it clear he did not think the British had anything to offer which he needed, his people were not so sure. Increasingly, the East India Company developed a highly lucrative traffic in opium, despite imperial bans first on importing the drug, then on smoking it.

War broke out after 20,000 chests of opium were destroyed, and a group of 350 foreign merchants confined to their factory compounds in an attempt by the Chinese to clamp down on the opium trade. The British government blockaded the Chinese ports, in the hope of exacting compensation. After a protracted period of fruitless negotiations, a fleet of twenty-five warships advanced up the Yangtze, taking strategic cities. Faced with the superior British firepower, the Chinese were forced to offer a package of agreements, which included the leasing of Hong Kong to the British as a trading base. But, of course, the ultimate irony of the whole episode was that they had been defeated by weapons that had originated in China, and were now coming back home again with a vengeance.

China's Great Wall may have offered only symbolic protection, but its romantic splendour made it a favourite subject for artists.

The lack of interest shown by the Chinese towards Britain's first diplomatic visit in 1792 is satirized in this cartoon by James Gillray. The ambassador, Lord Macartney, is seen kneeling at the head of a sycophantic delegation, some performing the ritual kowtow. The Emperor Quianlong seems to be concentrating on blowing smoke rings.

Quite apart from the immediate humiliation of defeat, the Chinese were faced with the longer-term consequences of their isolation from developments in military hardware. We have seen the importance of the steam engine in the early stages of the Industrial Revolution; what is less obvious is the debt the early steam engines owed to the technology of war.

The cannon can be seen as a kind of one-shot engine, with the gunpowder as the engine fuel, the cannonball as the piston, and the cannon itself as the cylinder. In both the cannon and the steam engine, a vital part of the manufacturing process is the creation of an airtight seal. So when the famous British ironmaster, John Wilkinson, pioneered a new way of boring a perfectly cylindrical channel through the barrel of a cannon, he took a step of critical importance for the steam engine. Such precision boring, allied to peacetime skills associated with clock-making and brewing technologies, made the steam engine possible (a fortuitous connection illustrated in Chapter One).

Once the *Rocket* had made its journey from Liverpool to Manchester, the pace of change was extraordinary. Within ten years, the *Rocket* itself was obsolete. Within a single generation, precision engineering was transforming industry of all kinds – and, as the machine revolution spread to North America, that new country increasingly stole the lead from the old.

An example of this is the story of the sewing machine. While British inventors had mechanized spinning and weaving, it was left to the Americans to come up with ways of mechanizing sewing. The crucial invention of the lockstitch was patented by Elias Howe in 1846. This meant that the machine used a double thread, instead of trying to imitate the sewing motion of the hand. But it was Isaac Merit Singer whose name became most widely associated with the sewing machine. His improved version was patented in 1851, the year of the Great Exhibition. Thanks to a combination of skilled engineering and successful marketing, annual production in the USA had risen to half a million by 1870.

The Singer sewing machine was remarkable not just as a machine, but as the first mass-produced consumer durable. If it broke down, it would still need the attention of a skilled fitter – but this, too, would change as the Americans made the next crucial breakthrough: the interchangeability of parts.

As Joel Mokyr, one of our historians, explains: 'Today, if something breaks down in your car, one of your spark plugs goes bad, you don't fix the spark plug, you take it out, you throw it away, you put in another one. You know that the new spark plug that you're putting in is going to be absolutely identical to the one you've just thrown away, except that the other one is broken and this one is fine. This is true for almost any mechanical part that we use today.

'Once again, this leads us to the technology of war, because the first successful attempt in producing interchangeability was in gun manufacturing, and it is perhaps no surprise that this should occur in a nation that has always loved guns.'

The extent to which the United States was outperforming Britain in the development of mass-production techniques was highlighted by displays of pistols at the Great Exhibition of 1851. The British gun-maker Robert Adams had hand-made prototypes, forged by skilled craftsmen from single pieces of iron. The American Samuel Colt had a large and impressive display of arms built up from a number of machine-made components. They had been produced by a relatively unskilled labour force, consisting largely of machine minders supervised by a few craftsmen.

'Britain was at that time the "workshop of the world", as they thought of themselves, and yet to their dismay they discovered that those damn Yankees could actually do things that

Singer's advertising stressed how simple their machines were to use – a claim that was reinforced with the development of interchangeable parts for easy repair.

THE FIRST LESSON ON THE SINGER Sewing Machine

THE NEW IMPROVED SINGER.
EASY TO USE — EASY TO LEARN — EASY TO BUY.

they couldn't do,' says Joel Mokyr. 'In particular it turned out Americans had become extremely good at building simple but highly accurate machine tools that of course eventually became the backbone of the interchangeable parts industry. It's inconceivable that somebody like Samuel Colt could have made the guns the way he did, at the price he did, of the quality he did, without his ability to cut those parts with a degree of accuracy and a level of tolerance that was beyond precedent.'

Samuel Colt's success in making his name synonymous with handguns was also due to skilful marketing and luck. The Mexican war of 1846 brought a government order for 1,000 revolvers, and within six years he had opened a manufacturing plant in England and another in Connecticut, capable of turning out 5,000 handguns a year. By the time he died, in 1862, he had sold nearly half a million weapons, and amassed a fortune equivalent to $300 million today.

Dramatic displays such as this one for an exhibition in New York in 1853 brought Colt's guns to the attention of an admiring public.

Mass production was an attractive proposition in America, where skilled labour was at a premium. It relied on the ingenuity of a very small number of clever engineers, who could produce a set of machine tools capable of achieving the right level of precision. Once an assembly line was tooled up, the day-to-day business of production was relatively simple. The social conditions were also favourable. This was a new, egalitarian society, where consumers did not necessarily care that their neighbours might also be buying an identical product.

'If you want custom-made clothes, a custom-made hunting rifle, where you're the only one who has one like that, then mass production isn't for you,' says Joel Mokyr. 'But in nineteenth-century America people were willing to buy goods as long as they worked well, as long as they were relatively inexpensive and as long as they were easy to maintain.'

With an increasingly prosperous economy at home, American presidents set their sights on becoming a power to be reckoned with abroad. Geography suggested an obvious target – Japan. Contact between Japan and the West had been limited to the few Dutchmen who were allowed to conduct trade from the island of Dejima, off Nagasaki. As we saw in the previous chapter, the shogunate had operated a deliberate policy of limiting Western influence.

However, the Japanese had become increasingly alarmed at the military strength demonstrated by the West against China during the period of the Opium Wars. When an American fleet sailed into Japan the message was clear: end the isolation, and open trade with the West. Having seen what had happened in China, the shoguns realized they had little choice. In 1854 they signed treaties with the United States, Britain, France, Russia and The Netherlands.

Up until this point, Japan had looked to China as the source of all important ideas; now, they realized that China was no longer the most significant power on Earth. There was a hunger to understand Western ideas, and to find out what they had missed. In this atmosphere, it was perhaps inevitable that the old guard should lose its influence; in 1867 the last shogun resigned, and a new regime came to power.

The Meiji Government was conservative in that it had an emperor at its head, but revolutionary in that it abandoned feudalism, and the old ordered class system. The samurai lost their ancient privileges, but were found posts in the new bureaucracy, in business, and in the modernized army and navy. Military conscription, the first railway, the Gregorian calendar, a ministry of education – even a daily newspaper – all arrived within the first five years of the new administration. By the turn of the century, Japan had undergone a dramatic social and industrial revolution.

How did it change so quickly? To answer this question, Alan Macfarlane has been studying the career of one man: Yukichi Fukuzawa. His portrait can be seen today on the 10,000 yen note – a fitting tribute to the man generally credited with convincing his fellow countrymen of the dazzling achievements of the West.

Fukuzawa was born in 1835 in Osaka, then the most prosperous city of Japan. His father, a samurai of lower rank, died when he was only one and a half, and the family was forced to return to his mother's remote rural area of Nakatsu. As a young samurai, Fukuzawa would normally have had a formal education in such 'essentials' as calligraphy and sword play, and would have been brought up to believe that manual labour was beneath him. However, by leaving Osaka at such a young age, he missed out on this – a 'loss' which, according to Alan Macfarlane, brought hidden benefits.

'Fukuzawa's early life as a poor samurai developed his character in various ways,' says Professor Macfarlane. 'Not only did he take unusual physical exercise, pounding rice and chopping wood, but he developed a keen interest in practical, do-it-yourself activities of a humble kind. Poverty and pride combined to make Fukuzawa a practical and versatile workman, a Japanese Benjamin Franklin, which later stood him in great stead when he came to study Western technology and science.'

Fukuzawa in Samurai dress on a visit to St Petersburg, Russia, in 1862. This portrait is held by the University at Keio, which he founded.

In his autobiography, Fukuzawa described how he grew to hate the inequality and hypocrisy of the feudal system, which he blamed for his father's early death. Perhaps because his family were already viewed as outsiders in the area where they lived, he became impatient with what he saw as pointless conventions. Samurai were not expected to handle money, and it was considered humiliating for them to be seen shopping for themselves – even if they could not afford to keep servants. Fukuzawa despised such mock gentility, and refused to follow the convention of wrapping his face in a towel and going out after dark whenever he had an errand to do.

When his brother asked him what he intended to be in the future, he replied that he would like to be the richest man in Japan, and spend all the money he wanted to. This clashed dramatically with the kind of conventional professions of loyalty to family and master that would have been expected. Fukuzawa questioned every-thing – these ties of loyalty included. When he was twelve or thirteen he accidentally stepped on a document naming his clan lord. His brother told him off and, though he apologized, he felt angry.

Then I went on, reasoning in my childish mind that if it was so wicked to step on a man's name, it would be very much more wicked to step on a god's name; and I determined to test the truth.

So I stole one of the charms, the thin paper slips, bearing sacred names, which are kept in many households for avoiding bad luck. And I deliberately trampled on it when nobody was looking. But no heavenly vengeance came.

'Very well,' I thought to myself. 'I will go a step further and try it in the worst place.' I took it to the chozu-ba [the privy] and put it in the filth. This time I was a little afraid, thinking I was going a little too far. But nothing happened.

'It is just as I thought,' I said to myself. 'What right did my brother have to scold me?' I felt that I had made a great discovery! But this I could not tell anybody, not even my mother or sisters.

Fukuzawa's father had wanted him to be a monk, as this was one way of circumventing the rigid social hierarchy. Such a path did not appeal to the young sceptic, although he was attracted by the idea of education. He started to attend school at the age of fourteen or fifteen – but his big chance came after the appearance of American warships off the coast of Japan. Suddenly, there was an urgent call for people who were prepared to learn Dutch – 'sideways writing' – in order to enable Japan to catch up with Western military developments. Fukuzawa was on the road to Nagasaki at the first opportunity. As he put it: 'I would have been glad to study a foreign language or the military art or anything else if it only gave me a chance to go away. ... I still remember how I swore to myself that like a bullet shot out of the gun's muzzle I would never come back. This was a happy day for me. I turned at the end of the town's street, spat on the ground, and walked quickly away.'

Within a year, he had left Nagasaki for a school in Osaka which had become a magnet for young people wanting to learn more about Western science and technology.

'They learnt Dutch in order to learn physics, biology, chemistry – they were trying to catch up with the whole of Western learning of some 200 years,' says Alan Macfarlane. 'He tells how he worked day and night. He used to go to sleep on his desk with his head pillowed, and then just wake up and keep working.'

A key problem was that the school had only one big dictionary and a dozen or so other books to work from. On one occasion, the school's director, Koan Ogata, managed to borrow a physics book from a visiting nobleman. Newly translated from English into Dutch, it was over a thousand pages long. The students seized on this book – but were forced to admit that copying it wholesale was impractical. Instead, they settled for the final chapter, a 300-page section on Faraday and electricity. They stayed up day and night until they had finished: one group sharpening the pens, another group making the ink, a third group copying. As a result, students from Ogata School became famous throughout the country for their expertise in electricity.

Fukuzawa did not realize the implications of the fact that this valued book was a translation from English into Dutch until he moved to Tokyo in 1858. On a visit to Yokohama, he was in for a shock: 'I had been striving with all my powers for many years to learn the Dutch language. And now when I had reason to believe myself one of the best in the country, I found that I could not even read the signs of merchants who had come to trade with us from foreign lands. It was a bitter disappointment, but I knew it was no time to be downhearted.'

Undaunted by the fact that he had devoted all his energies to learning the wrong language, he set about teaching himself English. This made him invaluable as one of the few Japanese people who could speak both languages. He was invited to join the first Japanese mission to America, and this was later to be followed by a visit to Europe. He was given official tours of buildings and institutions; in Britain, he visited a Newcastle coal mine, the Houses of Parliament, the Crystal Palace, Woolwich Arsenal and London Zoo.

In his native country, he tried to re-create not only the institutions he had seen, but the spirit behind them. Impressed by the opportunities for networking offered by the London gentlemen's clubs, he founded the Kojunsha social club in Tokyo, which survives to this day. (A tribute if ever there was one to the crucial role of clubs as a forum for the exchange of ideas, as we saw in Chapter Two.) He started a high school which developed into the first Japanese university, Keio. He also helped to set up a modern police force, established one of the first Western-style banks, and founded a daily newspaper, *Jiji Shimpo*.

The plate by the entrance to the Kojunsha Club.

He realized that Japanese inhibitions about public speaking held back development, so he wrote a book on the art and built a Hall of Public Speaking where it could be practised. Opened in 1875, the interior of this is modelled on a New England church. To this day, Japanese people tend to be extremely shy about public speaking, especially if it involves debate or disagreement. Fukuzawa saw it as a vital part of Western democracy.

Fukuzawa was a visionary. He saw more clearly than most Westerners how an industrial society functioned. It was more than good engineering, or brilliant science, or wise investment, although all of these were vital to success. What mattered just as much were the informal links between ideas and money, the freedom to compete and share information at the same time, and the ability of entrepreneurs to succeed, whatever their background.

Japan had entered the nineteenth century as a nation so backward it had even abandoned the wheel. It had lived for much of its history in the shadow of imperial China – yet by the twentieth century it had industrialized so successfully that it succeeded in beating its once powerful neighbour in battle. The influence of charismatic characters such as Fukuzawa was obviously part of the story – but there were also social factors, as Christopher Cullen explains.

'Japan's a different place from China in many ways,' he says. 'In the first place, they were used to borrowing things from the outside world, because they'd got so much of their culture from China. Secondly, at the Meiji Restoration in 1868 in Japan, what happened was that the samurai class, who were supposed to be privileged under the old system, worked out that they would be better off doing away with those privileges and going Western.

'In China, on the other hand, the scholar gentry just had too much to lose and too little to gain from rapid modernization and change in the nineteenth century. So they did not choose, in their own self-interest, to take the route that the Japanese samurai class chose to take in their circumstances.'

Self-interest seems to have been a predominant theme of this chapter. We have seen the unexpected technological spin-offs of weapons developed to promote one country's interests against another. In the relatively peaceful pursuit of agriculture, we have seen how farmers have made animals and machines work for them, mainly to save their own backs. Mechanization has made a life of leisure possible for the favoured few – but there are still many countries for whom this prospect is a distant dream.

The rise and fall of Europe and Asia can be charted over a thousand years – but our story so far has left large sections of the globe untouched. The fortunes of other landmasses – South as well as North America, Africa and Australia – can be explained only by widening the time frame to 10,000 years. On this time scale geography, ecology and biology had a profound effect on which parts of the world would industrialize first. The perspective is global: from cave paintings to mass communication, and from the hunter–gatherer to the shuffling queues in search of a polystyrene-packed Big Mac.

Chapter Six

ANIMAL FARM

All animals are equal but some animals are more equal than others.

GEORGE ORWELL: ANIMAL FARM (1945)

Searching for the roots of the Industrial Revolution on a 10,000-year time scale may seem like a perverse exercise. What possible connection could there be between the end of hunter–gatherers and the events that led to Fanny Kemble's journey on the *Rocket*? The answer is that the first seeds of capitalism can be traced back to the Neolithic Revolution when hunter–gatherers stopped roaming and settled down to grow crops and look after animals. For most of our history we have been hunter–gatherers. We moved around in small bands, hunting game and gathering wild plants. We lived off the land in harmony with nature. This most idyllic form of human existence finds an echo in the Bible as the Garden of Eden.

The exodus from Eden has been seen as a deep cultural memory of the end of hunter-gatherers. The change to settled agriculture did little to improve the quality of life. It resulted in a less varied diet, longer working hours, more toil, greater stress and terrible diseases. The enslavement of animals led to the enslavement of human beings. We were no longer equal. Some people were more equal than others. Slavery, avarice and conflict were some of the unfortunate consequences of our new way of life.

Homo sapiens began to develop a unique ability to change the natural world to meet human needs. We have adapted plants, animals and fossil fuels to meet the increased demands of a rising population. Over the past century the process has advanced so quickly that we might soon be in a position where we can even control our own evolution. The 10,000-year story of the quest to control nature takes us on a path from the domestication of animals to an icon of mass consumption: the

Hunter–gatherers poised for the kill, carved in stone.

McDonald's hamburger. This way of living and attitude to life, which began in the West, has now spread across the world.

In Des Plaines, an outer suburb of Chicago, historian Joel Mokyr visited a small drive-in restaurant that has become a shrine to the patron saint of fast food – the original founder of McDonald's, Ray Kroc. There is no food here. The waiter, French fries and burgers are all made of plastic. Kroc's big idea is frozen in time on the site of the first McDonald's restaurant. Today McDonald's feeds 32 million customers every day in 117 different countries around the world. Even India, where the cow is sacred, recently gave in when McDonald's promised the lamb burger. Since the first McDonald's restaurant opened in 1955, food has moved faster and faster. It is part of a much wider phenomenon, as Joel Mokyr explains.

'The essence of sustained technological progress is the disruption of harmony with nature,' he says. 'We want to keep disrupting it; that is the Western way of doing things.' And those who follow the Western way are rich, while everybody else is not. 'If you are going to live in harmony with nature you may be happy, but you are going to be poor. If you are going to be like the West then you are continuously disrupting nature, you are continuously causing ecological imbalances, and that is a very high price to pay. But it's a price that until now we have been willing to pay and we are still paying.

The first McDonald's hamburger restaurant – a milestone of the fast food era.

'Think about the road that humanity has travelled over the last 10,000 years. We have come down from small groups of hunter–gatherers to very, very large groups who dine at McDonald's. Has it been an improvement? Is this in some sense better? Has it all been for the best? I think we are going to disagree about that.'

So far this book has explored why the Industrial Revolution began in an unpromising corner of Europe before spreading to the rest of the Continent and then to North America and other parts of the world. But bigger, more basic questions remain: why did Europe and Asia develop so much faster than the other continents? Why was Africa, where *Homo sapiens* first emerged, not the birthplace of the modern world? Why did the nation states of Europe not become colonies of a powerful African empire? Why did native Americans, Australians and Africans all become victims of a dominant Western culture? Today the main language in Peru is Spanish. The Inca language is not spoken in South America, let alone Spain. Throughout recent history the world has been ruled by Europeans and Asians. Why?

The answers to many of these questions lie in the forces that drove the transition from hunter to farmer in certain parts of the world. Agriculture probably began as a gradual process, with nomadic people returning to places where they had planted seeds from their favourite foods. Initially, this was more like gardening than farming, until they were faced with an ecological crisis: 10,000 years ago the human population in some areas of the Eurasian landmass was struggling for survival. Nature's larder of large animals and edible plants was running low. Hobby farming was no longer sufficient to sustain an increasingly dense population, so people began trying to adapt nature to human needs, by intensifying the farming methods.

We know from archaeological evidence that the first cereal crops and domestic sheep were cultivated in an arc of land stretching from Jordan to Iraq, which has become known as the Fertile Crescent. Parts of China, India and the area around the Mediterranean followed over the next few thousand years. Once humans changed over to this new style of life there was no turning back. It had a profound impact on the relationships between individuals. Some farmers were more successful than other farmers. Some families had more children than other families. Some groups became more important than other groups, and people found their place in an increasingly hierarchical society. Once food supplies were stockpiled, it freed a small number of people to engage in other activities such as pottery and weaving. Gradually their technology and ideology changed. Over the next few thousand years the first villages and towns appeared. Food surpluses led to markets. Markets led to trade, and soon more complex societies emerged. The general picture is not difficult to grasp. The enormous social and economic diversity is much harder to explain.

What are the fundamental factors that have created these differences? The number of people an area can support will affect their survival strategy. If a region is sparsely populated with humans, but generously endowed with wild animals, there will be little pressure to start farming. This was the situation in sub-Saharan Africa where hunter–gatherers continued. If, on the other hand, an ecological crisis has created a lush river valley surrounded by inhospitable desert, the restricted hunting area may force hunter–gatherers to settle. The best survival option was to attempt to control the environment by farming crops and domesticating wild animals.

In *Animal Farm* George Orwell created a dominant leader in the shape of a pig called Napoleon, who tried to coerce other animals to be his slaves. It is a story that might have been familiar thousands of years ago when early attempts to establish settled communities were made. If a Napoleon-like figure emerged in the wide open bush of Africa or Australia, and his peers did not like the idea of settling down and being bossed about, they could run off into the night. Imagine the same thing happening in the river valleys of the Tigris or the Euphrates which are surrounded by desert on one side and mountains on the other. There was no escape from the Fertile Crescent. If they ran away, they would die. They were better off looking after the animals.

Historian Alan Macfarlane's house in the Nepalese village of Thak (in the lower half of which is a stable containing a couple of buffalo) is a good place to contemplate the role of domesticated animals in the evolution of society. He himself has an unusual way of looking at *Homo*

The 'peace' panel from the Royal Standard of Ur shows the variety of domestic animals in Mesopotamia in the third millennium BC. It was excavated from a ransacked tomb in the Royal Cemetery of Ur (in present-day Iraq) and is now on display at the British Museum.

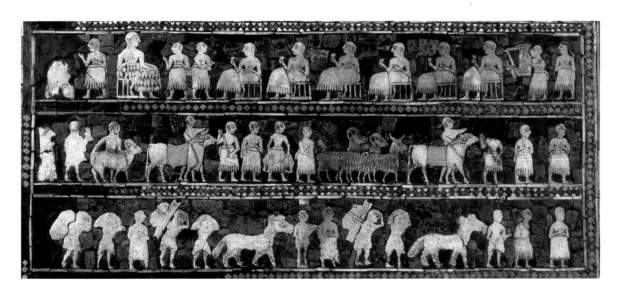

sapiens' relationship with animals. He sees humans as rather pathetic, limited creatures lacking claws, feathers, wings, fur or sharp teeth. They cannot run very fast and they have relatively poor eyesight, smell and hearing. However, they do have one important advantage – a large brain – and by harnessing tools they have made their way in the world. Alan Macfarlane's concept of a tool as an extension of the human body extends to animals, not just as biochemical engines to pull ploughs and carts, but as food processors.

As he feeds some large leaves to the animals beneath his house, he explains that the buffalo is an extension of the human stomach. If a human being attempted to eat such leaves, acute indigestion would soon follow. Our stomachs cannot digest cellulose, whereas the buffalo with its huge intestinal system can convert the fodder into four useful things for human beings: buffalo milk and buffalo dung while it is alive, and buffalo meat and buffalo hide when it is dead. It is an example of how an animal is used by human beings as a machine for converting energy from the hillsides and forests for use in the village and the rice terraces below.

The economics of domesticating animals are complex. The costs can outweigh the benefits of these walking 'tools'. The first farmers gradually learned how to breed animals selectively to fulfil a number of needs from carrying loads, to tilling land, to providing food. Even after the animals died, their skins could be used for leather coats and shoes. The most useful animals have always been big mammals. The first to be domesticated were sheep, goats and pigs; then cows, horses, donkeys and water buffaloes. One of the most difficult questions is why domestication of these animals occurred in some areas of the world and not others. In the Near East and China animal farming flourished, whereas in sub-Saharan Africa, the Americas and Australia hunter–gatherers continued alongside very limited agriculture. The only species domesticated outside Europe and Asia was the llama and alpaca in South America. So what was happening? Was it the people, the animals or the environment that created these differences?

The most likely answer is all three. We have seen how the surrounding landscape, climate and increased population density can force hunter–gatherers to settle, but perhaps the choice of animals available for domestication could also have an effect.

An animal audit across the planet 10,000 years ago would reveal obvious differences in the density and variety of species. Africa and Eurasia had the biggest selection of animals; whereas Australia and the Americas had been stripped of many of their larger mammals. One possibility is that severe climate changes caused mass extinction of the larger animals. A more likely explanation is that when humans arrived on these continents, between 12,000 and 50,000 years ago, these animals, which had evolved without human predators, were hunted to death.

Compare this to the situation in sub-Saharan Africa where animals evolved alongside hominids over millions of years. As hunting skills gradually improved, the faster, more evasive animals dominated the gene pool. So perhaps animals in Africa became more wary of human beings, whereas in Australia their experience of two-legged predators came too late in their evolution for survival tactics to evolve. After Australia's large animals had been decimated, the human population had few options for survival. The ecology of Australia was unsuitable for intensive farming, so the aboriginal people survived by continuing to hunt small marsupials. They gathered nuts and fruit and sometimes burned small areas to encourage new vegetation, but there were few settlements and no animals that could be domesticated.

In sub-Saharan Africa the plains were teeming with elephants, giraffes, zebras, rhinos – over fifty prime mammalian candidates. In Eurasia there were even more species – over seventy big mammals. These two continents shared the largest number of animals, yet on one continent animals were domesticated, while on the other they remained wild.

Genetically, zebras and horses are close relations. The ecological niche taken by the horse in central Asia is taken by the zebra in Africa. There were no horses in Africa, but why was its close cousin, the zebra, not domesticated? One explanation is that the animals filling the ecological niches on these two continents varied in their suitability for domestication. To be suitable for domestication an animal must fulfil a number of criteria: it must grow quickly, consume food efficiently, breed well in captivity and

The spread of the first humans from Africa to the rest of the world.

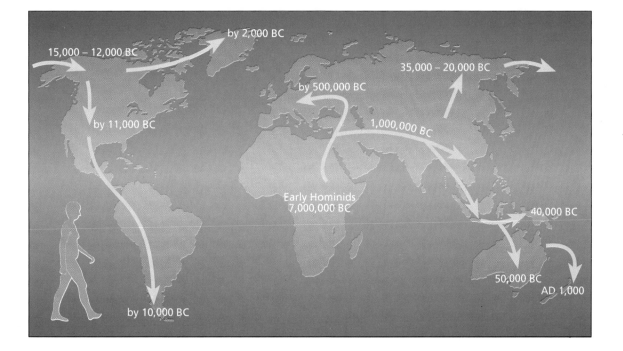

15,000 – 12,000 BC

by 2,000 BC

35,000 – 20,000 BC

by 500,000 BC

by 11,000 BC

1,000,000 BC

Early Hominids 7,000,000 BC

40,000 BC

50,000 BC

AD 1,000

by 10,000 BC

have a relaxed attitude to humans. Perhaps it is in this last category that the zebra failed. Attempts have been made to harness zebras to carts, but they have not been very successful. Most zookeepers will confirm that zebras can turn into bad-tempered beasts as they get older. When they bite, they tend not to let go.

So it is possible that the lack of domestic animals in North America, Australia and sub-Saharan Africa can be explained by mass extinctions and genetic suitability. When domestic animals did eventually arrive in these continents, thousands of years later, they were often quickly adopted. Bantu farmers in West Africa enjoyed enormous advantages over hunter–gatherers when they started to acquire sheep and cattle. Gradually over 1,000 years they dominated most of sub-Saharan Africa. Similarly, in North America there were no horses but, once the Great Plains Indians acquired them from European settlers, they became expert horse wranglers and eventually highly proficient horse-mounted warriors. This is further evidence that on these continents domestication was not determined by the attitude of the indigenous people, but by the lack of suitable indigenous animals to domesticate.

However, not everyone is convinced by this theory. Alan Macfarlane believes that the question is not so much if animals are suitable for domestication, but if people benefit from keeping them. He draws on his experience of Nepal. In Thak there has been a steady decline in the number and variety of domestic animals. When he first came to the village thirty years ago there were huge herds of buffaloes grazing in the forest. People are now unwilling to live alone in the forests and the cost of keeping animals has risen steeply. There used to be pigs in the village. Only the lowest caste can rear pigs – they are considered ritually impure by the higher-caste families. And eventually, under pressure from these families, the black pigs that used to live in Thak disappeared too. There used to be horses, but they left when the rich people who owned them moved out of the village. The horses were symbols of prestige. They were no use for ploughing because they would cause too much damage to the rice terraces. They were no use for riding because the terrain is too steep and rocky. So there was really no point in having horses. Mules can cope with the steep gradients of the paths, but generally it is cheaper to hire humans to carry loads. So there are ritual, social and economic reasons which force people into the decision of whether to have animals or not.

There is a further explanation for the uneven spread of domesticated animals across the continents. Within Europe and Asia the first places to domesticate animals were Mesopotamia (now part of Iraq) and China, but after a few thousand years animals were being domesticated across the entire continents in India, the Mediterranean and northern Europe. Europe and Asia may have had geographical advantages over the other continents which facilitated not just the spread of live-stock and crops, but also the diffusion of ideas and inventions. In *Guns, Germs and Steel*, a book that examines the disparity between the continents, Jared Diamond suggests that the shape and orientation of a continent may be significant. Eurasia has an east–west orientation and therefore its inhabitants share the same length of day and the same seasonal variations. They also tend to have similar climates and habitats. So when plants and animals spread horizontally across from the Fertile Crescent, they were already well adapted to their new habitats. Conversely, the continents of Africa and the Americas, which have a vertical, north–south orientation, straddle the Equator and are divided by a hot tropical barrier.

North–south diffusion across continents was much more difficult. Domestic crops and animals spread from Asia and Europe into Africa as far as Egypt and North Africa, but any further south and the climate was tropical. This north–south barrier extended 2,000 miles. There is a further disadvantage. Not only is the tropical ecosystem unable to support crops that thrive in a Mediterranean climate, but it allows organisms that may be lethal to livestock to thrive. For example, the reason the horse did not survive south of the Equator was its vulnerability to tropical diseases such as trypanosome caused by the tsetse fly.

The steep terrain of the rice terraces surrounding the village of Thak in Nepal.

The Americas were divided by a similar barrier created by the tropical forests of central America. Most domesticated crops and animals were not able to cross from north to south. Llamas and guineapigs that had been domesticated in the cool highlands of the Andes could not make it to the cool highlands of Mexico, because of the hot lowlands of central America. These geographical and climatic factors played an important part in limiting the spread of domestic animals across Africa and the Americas.

The only landmass with a complete set of farm animals that could breed and spread across the entire area was Eurasia. The global impact of those animal farms would be felt thousands of years later. Europeans and Asians had access to more energy, higher-yielding plants and superior breeds of animals, and they could travel faster on horseback. This unique combination gave Eurasia a huge economic advantage over the rest of the world.

Food surpluses generated enough wealth to enable some villagers to dabble in new technologies such as pottery, weaving and metal working. As villages became more prosperous, more people were needed to make things and eventually cities emerged. Human beings began to control other human beings. A class-based hierarchy evolved which led to serfdom, slavery and military rule. When the emerging states grew larger, laws and taxation systems were introduced.

Trade became an increasingly important part of city life. Originally this was carried out by exchanging one set of goods for another, but eventually credit lines and money were used. It was not long before officials and merchants needed to keep track of these transactions. The first written words were probably not the work of poets or philosophers, but the more prosaic scribbles of accountants, as Alan Macfarlane explains.

'It's rather startling to realize that probably writing was invented basically as an accounting device, to ensure that when goods were exchanged, or when a piece of property changed ownership, there was a permanent record of this. And therefore it developed in purely practical ways as a memory device. But the implications of this were immense, because once you had a way of externalizing and preserving information, you could get complex bureaucracies beginning to build up. You could get states with taxation systems and marketing systems. ... Without writing you could not really develop beyond very small barter trade to the complex markets which are the underpinning of modern capitalist industrialization.'

It is no coincidence that writing emerged in the same areas where the domestication of plants and animals began. The first words were written around 5,000 years ago in Mesopotamia in the Fertile Crescent. The only other places where writing started independently, without influence from other cultures, were Mexico and possibly China and Egypt. Mexico was isolated from the rest of the world, so once again Eurasia's geographical position enabled it to take advantage of this powerful tool. Writing spread rapidly. From primitive marks in clay to abstract phonetic characters on paper, writing evolved to serve the increased demands of trade.

Today we assume reading and writing is for everyone but, when writing was first introduced, it was intended for use by a privileged inner circle of scribes and rulers. They needed to record the number of animals each citizen had paid as taxes. If the writing system was complex, so much the better, it was a code with access restricted to those who needed to know. The anthropologist Claude Lévi-Strauss wrote that the main function of early writing was 'to facilitate the enslavement of other human beings'.

At the historians' meeting in Cambridge, Christopher Cullen showed an early form of contract written on a cuneiform clay tablet with a reed pen. It dates from 1300BC and records a commercial transaction for the sale of a young slave woman for forty-three pieces of silver.

'This thing is baked. It stands as a record. We're not any longer dependent on someone's memory of whether the thing happened or not. We have a written record, which has come down to us today, if we wanted to dispute the legality of the sale of this poor young woman, we certainly could. And it marks an immense transition in human society when you can create records independent of what there is in people's heads, the songs they can remember and lists of ancestors they can recite. So writing is something we have to think about as being absolutely crucial in certain deep societal changes that come not too long after the development of urban civilizations based on settled agriculture.'

The transformation of spoken language into written symbols took several different forms. The ancient civilizations around the Mediterranean used an alphabetic system for recording the different sounds of human speech. By learning twenty or thirty signs it was possible to read back the text of what someone had said. In the eastern half of Eurasia, in China, a more complex system emerged by the second millennium BC. This was based not on the sounds of the language, but on a large set of symbols, each one roughly corresponding to an object or idea. Learning to read and write this language was difficult because of the thousands of different symbols. To read a Chinese newspaper today requires knowing over 5,000 characters, and some of the bigger Chinese dictionaries have tens of thousands of characters. Written language in Japan is even more complicated because in addition to the Chinese characters the Japanese use two syllabaries called Katakana and Hiragana, which represent spoken syllables. So a Japanese newspaper mixes three different sets of symbols.

So what effect did the complexity of these written languages have on the development of the East? Initially, reading and writing were skills confined to the imperial courts; but gradually schools became popular with pupils who had ambitions to join the civil service. Literacy rates became surprisingly high and by 500 years ago 70 per cent of China's population were able to read and write.

As Christopher Cullen points out, the young human mind has proved itself flexible enough to learn almost any writing system human beings have created.

'Our emphasis on the wonder of the alphabetic system is perhaps another piece of our Eurocentrism. Dr Johnson in the eighteenth century was, in his perverse way, arguing against the popular notion that China must be a superior culture by saying: "Well, sir, they've not invented an alphabet, have they? They have not done what others could do. It shows they must be inferior in that respect." But it does not look as though this form of writing has quite the practical consequences people would claim.'

Learning the art of calligraphy was part of the drive to expand Confucian scholarship in order to select the brightest mandarins. In addition

Confucius, the philosopher whose teachings dominated the lives of the scholar-officials who formed the ruling class in China. Confucian doctrine was designed to preserve the status quo: 'Let the ruler rule, the minister administer, the father be a father, the son be a son.'

to being part of high culture, writing was crucial for the control of the extensive trade network. China became the most successful and powerful trading nation in the world and it would remain so for over a thousand years.

On the 10,000-year time scale China's supremacy is unrivalled. Some oriental scholars believe that Western domination over the past couple of centuries is a mere blip in the grand scheme of things. They think that the West has consistently underestimated the scope and scale of Eastern achievement. They believe east Asia is about to recover its traditional dominance of the world economy, with China resuming its normal position at the centre of the world stage.

In previous chapters we have already described how the Chinese were victims of their own success. They did not need ideas, or goods, or food from other countries. They were self-sufficient, stable and successful. This attitude of quiet confidence encouraged contentment and conservatism, but did not lead to innovation or radical ideas.

The potential of writing to influence society increased dramatically with the advent of printing. This technology seemed to amplify the cultural differences between East and West. In Europe, Gutenberg and his movable type triggered a shock wave that has been described as the gunpowder of the mind. In China it had a more limited effect, more like adding oil to a well-lubricated machine. Yet paper and printing were both invented in China.

Before the invention of paper the emperor had important texts transcribed on to silk, but most writing was inscribed on thin strips of bamboo or wood. The first paper was made in the second century AD from pulping mulberry bark, silk rags and other fibres. Over the next few hundred years it replaced wood and silk. Books were copied on to long thin scrolls and then wound on to rollers for storage.

The Confucian classics were engraved on large stones so that scholars could ink them and make paper copies. This was the earliest form of printing in China. The next breakthrough came with woodblock printing, which began in the eighth century. Letters were carved in reverse on to a wooden block, which was then inked and pressed against paper sheets. Printing was also used to produce legal documents and paper money. (Some of the first examples of counterfeit money entered

circulation in the Ming dynasty.) But the main impact of printing on Chinese society was to widen the availability of Confucian texts.

Printing spread across Eurasia through India, Persia and Egypt until it eventually reached Europe in the mid fifteenth century. European craftsmen began experimenting with presses and movable type. Books were printed in local languages and this helped establish a sense of identity for the emerging nation states in Europe. It also enabled Protestant dissidents, notably Luther, to split the Church. Printing encouraged the development of skilled craftsmanship and it became one of the first industries to divide work into specialized jobs. The compositor, the plate-maker, the ink-maker and the printer each learned a separate skill. The printing press also helped lay the foundations of another basic principle of mass production: it was one of the first machines to use interchangeable parts. In a sense the print works was a factory producing identical goods but, instead of making clothing, it was mass producing ideas.

Alan Macfarlane believes that the arrival of the printed book in Europe had a deep effect on people's perceptions of themselves.

'Before, you interacted with other people. You heard the news from other people. But everything was passed on by the spoken word. The

Calligraphy and ink drawing on paper, mounted on silk.

printing press gives you a book and you become an individual closed in the private space when you read. Some people think that the curious development of Western individualism, where I am I, you are you, and we are very different, each with our own private mental world, is somehow related to book reading. ... At first printing just looks like bits of metal which you put into a tray and print, but the side-effects on politics, economics, religion and the perception of the individual are vast – a revolution indeed.'

It is hard to imagine how the Renaissance, the Reformation, the Scientific Revolution and ultimately the Industrial Revolution could have happened without printing. The puzzle is why printing did not have the same impact in the eastern half of Eurasia. Alan Macfarlane suggests that printing emphasizes the social trends that are already present. In Europe there was a wide variety of linguistic, cultural and political differences which were reinforced in print. In China and Japan individual ideas were not tolerated, so printing bolstered the centre and crushed any ideological deviation. In the West there was an expansion of new knowledge; in the East there was recycling of the old dogma.

Printing in China was used to extend government mind control of the educated classes in the country. Every aspiring civil servant had to commit to memory long sections of the Confucian classics which were available from book shops. As the catalogue of books was rather limited and they had long print runs, it made economic sense to use wood blocks rather

Reconstruction of metal typesetting at Robert Smail's Printing Works in Innerleithen, Scotland.

than movable type. This kind of printing was more like stamping. The technology was cheap and required little investment, but once a block was made it was difficult to change.

Printing in Europe, on the other hand, was a cut-throat business. Every printer was eager to recoup the cost of his expensive printing press as Christopher Cullen explains.

'If you were a printer in Europe, you were desperate to find new and exciting books to print. If someone came to you and said I've got a book that is really going to excite everybody, you might well be prepared to advance that man money and have a sales network to distribute this book quickly round Europe. So if you are a subversive religious thinker, you might well find a printer very willing to put your book out because it would be a hot seller.'

Movable type allowed an entirely different relationship with truth, because it could always be changed or updated. It was originally invented in Korea, but movable type never really caught on in China and Japan until much later. It is not difficult to see why. Setting up a line of type using thousands of characters, rather than twenty-six letters, was a tedious, time-consuming business.

Later, after mechanical typewriters had been invented in the West, there was an even greater problem. How could you have a keyboard with thousands of characters? The 'QWERTY' keyboard had been designed with an intentionally awkward layout to slow down typing speeds in order to prevent letters colliding with each other as they struck the page. It was a difficult enough engineering problem with twenty-six letters converging on a single spot. With thousands of characters it was impossible. A solution was found, but you would not want to enter a speed-typing contest with this machine. Using a miniature arm, like an overhead crane, the operator had to scan a large tray of type containing thousands of metal characters. Having found the right one, it was picked from the tray, struck against the paper and then automatically returned to its location in the sea of type. A typist needed the eyesight and coordination of a cormorant diving for a fish each time a new character was selected.

So the mass communication of ideas in the Chinese language presented practical difficulties, even if the government had wanted to widen knowledge and print new titles. In Europe the expansion of ideas can to some extent be gauged by the number of books published each year. In 1600 there were 2,000 titles printed. By 1800 there were 20,000 new books published every year across Europe. There were maps, field guides, textbooks and tables.

Alan Macfarlane points to the tremendous advantage this gave Europe, not just in widening scientific knowledge, but also in gaining information about other civilizations.

Printing Chinese text from individual characters required a vast library of around 8,000 different pieces of moveable type. (These three characters mean 'cashmere goat'.)

'There was an enormous curiosity in Europe. One of its distinctive features, as well as its war-like nature and its competitiveness, was its curiosity. It always wanted to know about what was happening on the edges. After Columbus and other gallivantings round the globe, travellers often went with notebooks and wrote things down. They brought back ideas about new ways of doing things and these were put into books and then people all over Europe read about them. This was very different to what was happening in other parts of the world. While the West was absorbing the knowledge of all the other civilizations, the other civilizations were either closing themselves off or were not very interested.'

Within Europe, England was undergoing extraordinary growth compared to the rest of the Continent between 1600 and 1800. During this time the agricultural output per man, and per acre, was roughly double that of other countries in Europe. Although the population tripled during this period, the area of land used for agriculture did not increase significantly. So how did this happen?

The short answer is: animals. Improved crops and better tools were important, but what really distinguished English farming from continental farming was the quantity and quality of the livestock. The widespread use of animal power meant that the average agricultural worker in England could provide enough food for his family and two other families; whereas his French counterpart could only support half a family in addition to his own. A vast army of animal slaves was being harnessed by the English. There were many more horses in England compared to the rest of Europe, where the slower, less efficient ox was still widely used.

The puzzle is how a small, densely populated island could afford so many animals, especially as most parts of Europe were killing off their animals to use the land for arable farming. Again, there is a short answer: coal. While other European countries still relied on timber as their main energy source, coal was playing an increasingly important role in fuelling the furnaces and factories of Britain. This meant that land, which might otherwise have been used for growing forests, could be used for pasturing animals. By mining energy from the ground, harnessing animal power in the fields and freeing human labour for the mills the stage was set for the Industrial Revolution. The urge to take control of nature and use the resources to fulfil human needs spread to mainland Europe, and eventually across most of the world, as Joel Mokyr explains.

'What happened in Europe, in particular in western Europe, is that slowly but certainly people came to the realization that in fact the manipulation of the physical world is nothing to feel guilty about. In fact if you manipulate nature you are only illustrating the glory of the Creator. If the Creator in his infinite wisdom has created something and put us in the middle of it and put it at our disposal, this is a deep Judaeo–Christian presumption reflected in the Book of Genesis. And people I think truly believed it. I think our technological success is in large part due to the fact that we believe this entire physical environment is ours. We can do with it whatever we want and we can manipulate it for our own benefit.'

By 1492, Europe was a powerful civilization. Having harnessed human power, animal power, water power and wind power; Europeans were able to plough fields, grind grains, pulp paper, drive mills, saw timber, fire forges, blast furnaces and build ships that would eventually expand their control of the natural world to other continents. No other continent had this unique blend of knowledge, technical skill and political will. It is one thing to have the ambition to colonize the world, yet how did a few Europeans so effectively decimate the native populations of Africa, Australia and the Americas? The secret of their 'success' can be traced back to the farm animals they had reared for thousands of years.

The first link is indirect. Settled agriculture allowed some people to develop craft skills such as metal-working. Blacksmiths produced horse-shoes, bridles and stirrups, which turned horses into instruments of war. They also made daggers, swords and lances to equip the conquistadors. When Cortés crushed the Aztecs and Pizarro routed the Incas, they were able to slay thousands of Indians with a few dozen horsemen armed with superior weapons. The slingshots and clubs of the Indians had little effect

Three Prize Pigs. Breeding the perfect farm animal was an important part of the agricultural revolution in England. The omnivorous appetite of the pig made it the most efficient source of meat.

174

on the steel-armoured warriors. The battles were often won in the face of absurd numerical odds of 500 to one. Reports of these victories were written up, sent home, and read by future adventurers. They were able to learn from previous experiences and alter their plans accordingly. The Indian leaders, who were dispersed across a large continent, may have heard unreliable oral accounts of these massacres but, when confronted by European invaders, they were defeated by similar tactics.

Later, in the conquest of North America, guns became more important, but the most lethal weapon the European invaders possessed was invisible and it had a much more direct link to the domestication of animals.

European infectious diseases spread through the native populations, killing hundreds of thousands of people. These diseases, such as smallpox, measles, tuberculosis and influenza, had been endemic in Europe for hundreds of years. Many of them were originally associated with domestic animals. They were often fatal in childhood, but children who survived had a natural immunity to the disease, which tended to be passed on to their offspring. Consequently, although these diseases were still dangerous, there was a gradual resistance to these pathogens in the European population.

Spanish conquistadors destroyed Aztec armies on horseback and used intrigue to induce civil war, but it was the import of European germs that completed the conquest of Mexico.

When European explorers set off to the Americas with their farm animals, they did not realize they were carrying a lethal cargo. The natives of the New World had no resistance to these diseases and the consequences were catastrophic. Some estimates suggest that up to 95 per cent of the pre-Columbian native people may have been wiped out by these diseases. The only germ that the pre-Columbian population probably inflicted on their European invaders was syphilis, an appropriate revenge for the rape and pillage of their continent.

Joel Mokyr thinks that the cultural and political organization of the Europeans was also pivotal to their success.

'The Europeans who ended up in America, the Cortéses and the Pizarros, had a certain ruthlessness, a certain aggression that I think is something these native people had not entirely encountered. There is a way in which the Europeans lie and trick these populations and disrupt their political structures. Also they could organize themselves in the sense of having incredibly long supply lines and still be able to continuously keep in touch with Europe and bring reinforcements when they needed them. It's not just about violence … there were people who were violent in a disorganized way, and people who were violent in an organized way; and the ones that were organized usually won.'

The English settlers who came to North America may not have been quite so brutal as the Spanish but, if the Indian tribes interfered with their settlements, they were driven away. Eventually, when the Indians acquired horses, they were quick to use them in battle. But the real war was not with bullets; once again it was microbes that inflicted the worst casualties. The tragedy of the immunological imbalance between Europeans and North American Indians continued into the nineteenth century.

An incident in North Dakota in 1837 demonstrates the horror of this unintentional biological warfare. Along the Missouri River a peaceful Indian tribe, called the Mandans, had settled in small villages constructed of huge earth igloos called earth lodges. They grew corn and vegetables and traded with the fur trading station at Fort Clark next door to their settlements. One day a paddle steamer called the *St Peter* came up the river to deliver supplies to the fort. Unfortunately, someone on board was carrying smallpox. The disease swept through the lodges and caused panic. Some people committed suicide when they feared they were going down with this horrific illness. It killed 90 per cent of the tribe, including their formidable chief, Four Bears. As he began to succumb to the symptoms he made a final speech to his people, transcribed by a fur trader in *Chardon's Journal at Fort Clark* (1837):

'Ever since I can remember, I have loved the Whites. … The Four Bears never saw a White man hungry … I was always ready to die for them, which they cannot deny. I have done everything that a Red Skin could do for them, and

The Mandan tribe protected themselves from Sioux raids by surrounding their villages with wooden stockades. Scalps of defeated warriors were mounted on tall poles to warn off attackers. The Mandans were always friendly with European settlers, but had no defence against the white man's diseases.

how have they repaid it! With ingratitude! I have never called a White Man a dog, but today I do pronounce them to be a set of black-hearted dogs. They have deceived me. Them that I have always considered to be brothers have been my worst enemies. I have been in many battles and often wounded, but the wounds of my enemies I exalt in. But today I am wounded. And by whom? By those same White dogs that I have always considered and treated as Brothers. I do not fear death, my friends. You know it. But to die with your face rotten, that even the wolves will shrink with horror at seeing me, and say to themselves, "That is the Four Bears, the friend of the Whites."'

While the native population of North America was being slowly wiped out and pushed into less fertile lands, one of the most massive human migrations in history was taking place. European immigrants were flooding into the New World. They brought with them all the benefits of centuries of technological achievement that dated back to their early domestication of animals.

There was one new kind of mechanical animal – the iron horse – which arrived in America the same year that the *Rocket* made its first journey on the Liverpool to Manchester railway. The 1830s was the beginning of a tremendous boom in railroad construction in Britain and North America. What few people can have realized is that the Industrial Revolution in Britain and the rest of Europe was just a foretaste of the immense wealth that could be unleashed by a capitalist economy. Now an entire continent was about to begin its colossal rise to power. The size of this continent, initially a disadvantage, was turned into an advantage by the railroad. The vast reservoir of natural resources from timber and coal to meat and wheat could be linked to the giant manufacturing centres. Economies of scale and mass production would make millions for the businessmen who invested their capital in the future of America.

A good example of this transformation was the growth of a small village on the shore of Lake Michigan called Chicago. By 1833 the last of the Indians had been driven out of the area. They had no concept of land ownership or property rights. Within a few years property speculation caused a thousand-fold increase in the price of land.

A French political scientist Emile Boutmy had this description of Americans in *Studies in Constitutional Law: France – England – United States* (1891): 'Their one primary and predominant object is to cultivate and settle these prairies, forests and vast waste lands. The striking and peculiar characteristic of American society is, that it is not so much a democracy as a huge commercial company for the discovery, cultivation and capitalization of its enormous territory. ... The United States are primarily a commercial society ... and only secondarily a nation.'

The Westward expansion of the railroad allowed the Great American Dream to begin. (Lithograph by Currier and Ives, New York, 1868.)

South and west of Chicago the prairies were being transformed into huge farms and ranches. Timber, meat and grain were shipped east through the Great Lakes, but in the winter months the lakes froze and Chicago was isolated.

The first stage in the solution of this problem was to build railroads that would bring cattle and grain to a central depot before sending them east. Farmers, anxious to avoid the mud bath of the wagon tracks leading into Chicago, pledged to buy stock in the new railroad companies. In the decade between 1850 and 1860, the total amount of track across America increased from 9,000 miles to 30,000 miles. The huge volume of goods shipped on the railroads created ruthless competition between companies. The freight routes with more than one line were often run at a loss to drive competitors out of business.

Chicago became the hub of a vast human enterprise to exploit the natural resources of America. The prairies were turned into wheat fields, the pine forests surrounding the Great Lakes were stripped for timber, the huge herds of bison that were the life blood of Plains Indians were slaughtered to make way for ranch cattle. In the history of the planet there can have been no faster change of land use from hunter–gatherers to settled agriculture. The Midwest had the potential to be the bread basket and meat platter of America. Immigrants were pouring into the industrial cities of the

Herds of bison, which had roamed the prairies for thousands of years, were decimated by the end of the nineteenth century. Millions were slaughtered when the railroad extended the market for their hides.

eastern states and they needed feeding. A new leap in the production and distribution of food was needed to ensure this rapidly expanding population did not go hungry.

Grain was no longer shipped around in sacks – it was moved around by automatic machinery. The invention of the grain elevator transformed warehouses into multi-storey factories, transporting grain from one bin to another by steam-powered conveyer belts. Lines of railroad cars were unloaded on one side, while ships were loaded on the other. The novelist Anthony Trollope, who visited a Chicago grain elevator in 1861, noted: 'It was not as a storehouse that this great building was so remarkable, but as a channel or a river course for the flooding freshets of corn. ... It is a world in itself – and the dustiest of all the worlds.'

Grain elevators were more than just automatic warehouses. They became like banks, but instead of depositing or taking out money, farmers and merchants were given receipts which could be exchanged on demand. The advent of the telegraph ensured that any change in prices could be communicated quickly across the nation and this created a new kind of market.

At the Chicago Board of Trade a futures market began to flourish with traders offering fixed-price contracts to protect people from price fluctuations in the future. The volume of business became staggering. By 1870 Chicago had become the biggest market in the world for lumber, grain, cattle and pigs. Food was no longer just something to be eaten or grown: it had become a commodity, and was now an integral part of the system of capital.

The industrialization of food reached new heights in Chicago with the opening of the Union Stock Yard in 1865. Within a few years the site had grown to over a hundred acres and on a single day could accommodate 21,000 head of cattle, 75,000 hogs and 22,000 sheep. This was carnage on a truly industrial scale – production-line butchery that became known as a 'disassembly line'. The carcasses were delivered on a rotating wheel to a long line of workers who each performed a specific act of butchery. The idea of the disassembly line originally came from the city of Cincinnati, the pig capital of America, which was nicknamed Porkopolis. On a visit to the city Frederick Olmsted, a famous landscape architect, gave this graphic account of the atmosphere inside a meat-packing plant in his *Journey through Texas* (1854):

A bird's-eye view of Chicago in 1857 by James Palmatary. It shows the railroad leading to the large grain elevators at the mouth of the Chicago river. Ships line the river which continues up into the warehouse and financial districts.

The Chicago Board of Trade — a temple of capitalism. Traders wishing to buy or sell gesticulated at each other across circular pits in the great hall. Behind the daily pandemonium was a highly lucrative futures market where speculators made and lost money predicting the rise and fall of commodity prices.

ILLINOIS. — THE GREAT HALL OF THE BOARD OF TRADE BUILDING, CHICAGO — SCENE DURING A SESSION OF THE BOARD.
FROM A SKETCH BY A STAFF ARTIST.

We entered an immense low-ceilinged room and followed a vista of dead swine, upon their backs, their paws stretching toward heaven. Walking down to the vanishing point, we found there a sort of human chopping machine where the hogs were converted into commercial pork. A plank table, two men to lift and turn, two to wield the cleavers, were its component parts. No iron cog wheels could work with more regular motion. Plump, falls the hog upon the table, chop, chop; chop, chop; chop, chop fall the cleavers. All is over. But, before you can say so, plump, chop, chop; chop, chop; chop, chop sounds again. … Amazed beyond all expectation at the celerity, we took our watches and counted thirty-five seconds, from the moment when one pig touched the table until the next occupied its place.

Pigs were easy to industrialize. The pork was salted, packed and dispatched on the railroad. Cattle presented a different problem, because customers liked to eat beef fresh. Anyone who could slaughter and dress beef in Chicago, yet deliver it fresh on to the plates of New York restaurants, could make a fortune. A Boston butcher, Gustavus Swift, came to Chicago and was one of many who tried to achieve this goal. He carried out an experiment – shipping two carloads of dressed beef to New England during midwinter in stripped-down railroad cars with their doors left open. The cold air moving across the meat led him to develop the refrigerator car. This made him his fortune and also spawned an entirely new industry – the manufacture of ice.

It meant that instead of shipping live steers by rail, beef could be processed and packed in the same way as pork. The new Swift meat-packing plant was a model of automated production, as Joel Mokyr explains: 'This process was extremely efficient and was based on a very high division of labour. I don't think Adam Smith in his wildest nightmares could have imagined anything like the Swift plant in Chicago.'

The meat disassembly line may have given Henry Ford the idea for his Model T car assembly line. His integrated system of blast furnaces, mines,

Illustrations from *Scientific American* (1891) describing the step-by-step process of dismantling pigs on a disassembly line.

manufacturing and sales offices became a model for the giant corporation of America. The boom in manufacturing was not the only factor responsible for the extraordinary economic growth of this nation. There were equally important developments in patterns of consumption. Chicago was the home of the mail order catalogue which changed the way goods were sold. The Montgomery Ward catalogue was an encyclopedia for the American consumer, selling everything from sausagemeat to complete houses. The 'Busy Bee Hive' where all mail orders were processed became a powerful symbol of modern urban life from the East Coast to the West.

Capitalism was in its rawest form in America. It seemed completely unstoppable. The Wall Street crash of 1929 and the Great Depression of the 1930s alerted people to the uncertainty and inequality of the great American dream. But the humanitarian alternative, Communism, enjoyed only short-lived popularity. For a brief period in the Soviet Union, Communism seemed to offer a more egalitarian way of distributing a state's wealth. In practice, however, it was an illusion. The system sunk into a quagmire of greed, corruption and lethargy. Perhaps in the 10,000-year view of history, Cmmunism may be viewed as just a footnote, an interesting idea, a worthwhile goal but, in the end, an experiment doomed to failure. It is still too early to tell. At the moment capitalism is the force that dominates the planet.

On the 10,000-year time scale the last two world wars may be seen as a continuation of the perpetual state of war that has existed between the

Repeating the same task hundreds of times a day was the essence of assembly line work. At this Henry Ford plant, the engines filed slowly past the workers as they added identical components to each one.

aggressive nations of Europe. There were two key differences between previous conflicts. First, industrialization introduced a new level of mechanization and destruction. Second, the colonization of large parts of the world by European nations made it inevitable that the entire world would be dragged into these wars. The Neolithic and Industrial Revolutions helped create these wars. It is tempting to imagine these conflicts, like many others since the end of hunter–gatherers, were predestined – but they were not.

Looking back over the last 10,000 years, Alan Macfarlane emphasized the accidental nature of history. Small differences between civilizations and chance discoveries caused unintentional, sometimes terrible, consequences that have led us to where we are today.

'There are many historians who think history is predestined still. They write as if at some point in time it had to happen like this. I think it never had to happen like this until yesterday, and today we don't know. No one predicted the fall of the Soviet Union, for example, the day before it happened. No one predicted the French Revolution and even through the middle of it no one knew it was happening. So it's all a game of chance and accident and unintended consequences.'

At the end of their discussions in Cambridge, the group returned to the question posed by Joel Mokyr at the beginning of the chapter: 'are we really any better off today than we were 10,000 years ago?'

Christopher Cullen remained unconvinced about our progress:

'I do feel very sceptical about the model of human beings marching towards sunlit uplands, as they become more and more civilized, and more technically able. What is it that we have gained from becoming agriculturalists and from later having more and more complex cities? I think that when we were hunter–gatherers we invented most of what really matters about being human. We invented our families, our language, our religion, music, dance, poetry, many of the really good things in life. And I'm not quite sure what we have gained since actually.'

"A BUSY BEE HIVE."
SECTIONAL VIEW OF THE ENORMOUS ESTABLISHMENT OF
MONTGOMERY WARD & CO.
MICHIGAN AVENUE, MADISON AND WASHINGTON STREETS, CHICAGO.

Montgomery Ward & Co. was the pioneer of mail-order shopping. By cutting out the middle men and doing away with shops the prices were unbeatable. This cover of the 1900 catalogue shows a cutaway of the 'Busy Bee Hive' from which orders were dispatched by railroad all over America.

Joel Mokyr was quick to dampen his enthusiasm by pointing out that he doubted whether hunter–gatherers could have painted the *Mona Lisa* or written the *St Matthew's Passion*. He continued his argument.

'Any calculation that tries to compare the living standards on the eve of the Industrial Revolution with those at the beginning of the Neolithic era strike me as just truly absurd. You're not comparing like with like. It may well be that during the time of the Renaissance, or the Roman Empire, or the Chinese Empire, human culture was enjoyed by a relatively small proportion of the population. And yet this is to some extent *Homo sapiens'* greatest creation. We're not just counting the number of teeth that hunter–gatherers have. We have left something to posterity which people visit in museums, listen to in concerts and read in libraries. And in that regard there is no question that the invention of agriculture and the urban society that it implied, produced something that would not have been produced in any other way.'

Maxine Berg reminded everyone of the point that Adam Smith had made: that the progress of the wealth of nations had made it possible for an ordinary labourer to live at a standard of living higher than an African prince of a Neolithic society. She thinks that it is people's desires and wants that pushes them into a consumer society and eventually industrialization: 'It's that shift in labour time within families, especially women's labour, into new activities, so that they go out to work for other people in order to buy beautiful clothes and ribbons and pottery and to live the civilized life that we want. It's not just the very rich who are having this, but the middle classes and the ordinary people too.'

Simon Schaffer felt uncomfortable 'sitting on the Martian judgement seat deciding which stage of human development looked best'. He talked about his suspicions of a theme that has persisted throughout the period of the Industrial Revolution associated with such figures as Jean-Jacques Rousseau. Rousseau rejected urban life in favour of a nostalgic vision of humankind plucking fruit from trees.

'Nostalgia is clearly a very often highly conservative, extremely distressing and almost always ill-informed account of what human purpose should be; but so is the complacency which identifies the immediate present with the best of all possible worlds. Just before Rousseau there is a character, who is viciously caricatured in Voltaire's *Candide*, Doctor Pangloss, who simply cannot imagine a better world than this one, because it was created by a mixture of reason and wisdom; and anything logically possible exists and in the best of all possible worlds what exists must be the best of all possible things.

'So somehow or other, between hopeless nostalgia and far too complacent affirmation of our present, I think those are the two great errors against which the history of the great industrial transformation should counsel us.'

Did the Neolithic revolution mark the end of an idyllic way of life?

Alan Macfarlane thinks that in some ways we are returning to a hunter–gatherer-like society.

'If you look at a great city like Chicago, or London or Tokyo, you'll find people who act like hunters and gatherers in many ways. They rush around, skimming not off nature, but off machinery and surpluses. They don't have to work with their bodies in the hard way that agricultural people had to work. ... You have a sort of social structure, and a way of life, which although it is technologically much more sophisticated, reminds me very much of hunters and gatherers. So in some ways it's been a sandwich history with the bread at the beginning and the bread at the end, and a sharp taste in the middle.'

This book began with a single day in 1830 and expanded to 10,000 years. The purpose of the exercise was not to suggest that the Industrial Revolution could have begun only in Britain or to indulge in triumphalism, but to look at the series of geographical, biological and social accidents that triggered the events on that island. Minor changes in circumstances could have resulted in a very different outcome. The seeds of industrialization have now spread round the world. On the wide time scales of the last few chapters it has been possible to see how many countries and cultures have contributed to the development of technologies we take for granted. Now we are seeing the emergence of global culture.

This is most obvious in the shopping malls of the developed world, but it is also visible in the aspirations and possessions of the growing middle classes in less developed parts of the world. This process of globalization will widen as more and more people have access to the outside world

Have we returned to being hunter–gatherers again, but in a different context?

through e-mail, e-commerce, e-entertainment and e-life. The global computer network has the potential to blur the division between New York and New Delhi, buyer and seller, writer and reader, movie fan and movie director. For example, the success of low-budget films such as *The Blair Witch Project* makes it seem possible that with word-of-mouth publicity, anyone with a little flair could go out, shoot their own film and show it to anyone in the world with a computer. If you wanted to see our film, your bank details would be fed to our bank, and for a modest fee our film would be downloaded on to your screen. And the same could happen in reverse, if we wanted to see your latest epic.

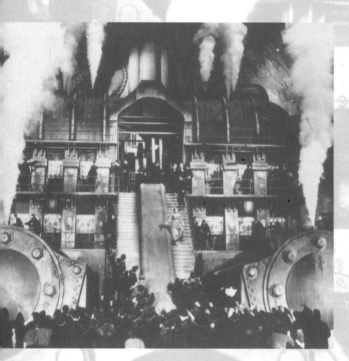

This vision of the future conjures up a picture of the end of corporate power, the decline of the nation state and the rise of the lone ranger. Many feel a deep distrust of corporations and are horrified by nationalism, yet feel powerless to do anything about it. The communications network is starting to change that. Instead of hunting food, the new hunters gather and exchange information from different territories around the world. Could this be the dawn of a new egalitarian era, where everyone has a chance to make their mark? Perhaps it is a return to the roots of our hunter–gatherer ancestors.

The idea of a return to Eden is an attractive dream, but like most predictions is probably a flawed fantasy. There are too many variables to be able to predict what follows the Neolithic and Industrial Revolutions; and too much uncertainty about what will happen to the poor half of the world that can barely afford food, let alone computers.

One thing is unlikely to change: the human need to understand, adapt and control the natural world. Over the last 10,000 years humans have harnessed energy from wind, water and animals; extracted energy from coal, oil and the nucleus of the atom; and we have controlled the breeding of crops and animals to feed our rising population. To cope with continued growth we are beginning to apply our new genetic knowledge to manipulate the genes of crops and animals to increase food yields. Perhaps there is only one thing left to control: ourselves. By manipulating our own genes we might be able to have direct control of our own evolution.

Alan Macfarlane thinks we may even create a new species. Perhaps *Homo sapiens* will evolve into *Homo artificialis*, a hybrid human with genetically selected biological systems interfacing with a variety of add-on features from enhanced memory storage to sensory inputs for mind adventures. Perhaps in the future you will be able to see a reconstruction of the first *Rocket* journey, not on a screen but inside your head. The problem with such predictions is imagining the wider implications of what it would be like to live in a society with such technology.

After Fanny Kemble rode on the *Rocket*, she described it as a 'snorting little animal'. In 1830 horses were the main form of transport across land, so it is not surprising she saw the machine in this way. Her entire concept of travel was altered by this journey, but even with this experience she would have been unable to predict the scale and speed

of change over the next couple of decades. Trying to predict a century ahead, she would have had even more trouble. She might have been able to imagine a car as a horseless carriage, but she could never have conceived of road networks with vast volumes of traffic or giant metal birds crowding the skies.

In *1984* George Orwell described a society dominated by television, with thought police monitoring the rewriting of history. It is a vision that haunts anyone who attempts to look back at the past, particularly as so much history seems to be rewritten to match current ways of thinking. Perhaps there is no way round this. History is, after all, telling stories of the past which make sense today. Stories of the future are the same. So the idea of a virtual hunter–gatherer, or a hybrid human, tells us more about where we are now, than where we will be in the future.

Metropolis. Fritz Lang's chilling vision of the year 2000 was inspired by a visit to New York in the 1920s.

FURTHER READING

GENERAL

Hobsbawm, E. J., *Industry and Empire*. Penguin, London, 1969

Jennings, Humphrey, *Pandaemonium*. André Deutsch, London, 1985

Macfarlane, Alan, *The Riddle of the Modern World*. Macmillan, London, 2000

Mokyr, Joel, *The Lever of Riches*. Oxford University Press, New York, 1990

Mumford, Lewis, *Technics and Civilization*. Harcourt Brace & Co, New York, 1934

Sellar, W.C. and Yeatman, R.J.: *1066 and All That*. Penguin, London, 1960

CHAPTER ONE: THE IRON HORSE

Burton, Anthony, *The Rainhill Story*. BBC Books, London, 1980

Cobbett, William, *Rural Rides*. Penguin, London, 1967

Malthus, T. R., *An Essay on the Principle of Population*. Penguin, London, 1970

Thomas, R. H. G., *The Liverpool and Manchester Railway*. Batsford, London, 1980

CHAPTER TWO: WHEELING AND DEALING

Berg, Maxine, *The Age of Manufactures 1700–1820*. Routledge, London, 1994

Briggs, Asa, *The Age of Improvement 1783–1867*. Longman, London, 1959

Engels, Friedrich, *The Condition of the Working Class in England*. Penguin, London, 1987

Macfarlane, Alan, *The Origins of English Individualism*. Blackwell, Oxford, 1978

Smith, Adam, *The Wealth of Nations*. Everyman, London, 1910

Trinder, Barrie, *The Making of the Industrial Landscape*. J. M. Dent, London, 1982

Trinder, Barrie (ed.), *'The Most Extraordinary District in the World'*. Phillimore, Ironbridge Gorge Museum Trust, 1997

Young, Hilary (ed.), *The Genius of Wedgwood*. Victoria and Albert Museum, London, 1995

CHAPTER THREE: SHIPS OF FORTUNE

Cobbe, Hugh (ed.), *Cook's Voyages and Peoples of the Pacific*. British Museum, London, 1979

Hepper, Nigel, *Kew: Gardens for Science and Pleasure*. HMSO, London, 1982

Jones, E. L., *The European Miracle*. Cambridge University Press, Cambridge, 1981

Parker, Geoffrey, *The Military Revolution*. Cambridge University Press, Cambridge, 1988

Sobel, Dava, *Longitude*. Fourth Estate, London, 1996

CHAPTER FOUR: THE HEAVENLY MACHINE

Agricola, Georgius (trans. Herbert Clark Hoover and Lou Henry Hoover), *De Re Metallica*. Dover, New York, 1950

Cronin, Vincent, *The Wise Man from the West: Matteo Ricci and his mission to China*. Fount, London, 1984

Harris, Nathaniel, *The Hamlyn History of Imperial China*. Hamlyn, London, 1999

Landes, David S., *Revolution in Time*. Harvard University Press, Cambridge, Mass., 1983

Macfarlane, Alan, *The Savage Wars of Peace*. Blackwell, Oxford, 1997

Needham, Joseph; *Science and Civilisation in China*. Cambridge University Press, Cambridge, 1954

Ying-Hsing, Sung (trans. and annotated by E-Tu Zen Sun and Shiou-Chuan Sun), *Chinese Technology in the Seventeenth Century*. Dover, New York, 1997

CHAPTER FIVE: WAR AND PEACE

Gies, Frances and Joseph, *Cathedral, Forge and Waterwheel*. HarperCollins, New York, 1994

Kiyooka, Eiichi (trans.), *The Autobiography of Yukichi Fukuzawa*. Columbia, New York, 1966

McNeill, William H., *The Pursuit of Power*. Blackwell, Oxford, 1983

Ruskin, John, *The Stones of Venice*. Da Capo Press, New York, 1960

Temple, Robert, *The Genius of China*. Prion Books, London, 1991

CHAPTER SIX: ANIMAL FARM

Cronon, William, *Nature's Metropolis: Chicago and the Great West*. Norton, New York, 1992

Diamond, Jared, *Guns, Germs and Steel: A short history of everybody for the last 13,000 years*. Jonathan Cape, London, 1997

Flannery, Tim, *The Future Eaters*. Reed, Victoria, 1994

Frank, André Gunder, *Re-Orient: Global economy in the asian age*. University of California, Berkeley and Los Angeles, 1998

Landes, David S., *The Wealth and Poverty of Nations*. Little, Brown, London, 1998

Pacey, Arnold, *Technology in World Civilization*. MIT, Cambridge, Massachusetts, 1991

ACKNOWLEDGEMENTS

The inspiration for this project came from a meeting with two remarkable Cambridge scholars, Alan Macfarlane and Simon Schaffer. We are indebted to them and to the other historians: Maxine Berg, Christopher Cullen and Joel Mokyr who generated many of the ideas on which the television series and this accompanying book are based.

During the course of the research we met a number of people who provided valuable insights and help including: Michael Bailey, Kent Deng, Sarah Harrison, Akira Hayami, Rob Iliffe, Ian Inkster, Eric Jones, Gerry Martin, Patrick O'Brian, Osamo Saito Saito and Mark Turin.

We owe special thanks to the Channel 4 Books' lively editorial team especially Emma Tait, the editor, and Christine King who made numerous suggestions for improving the text; Mark Wallace who assisted on the picture research; Isobel Gillan who designed the book and editorial director Charlie Carman.

At Channel 4 Television, commissioning editors Sara Ramsden and Charles Furneaux had faith in what sometimes seemed an over-ambitious, wacky idea. A project on this scale normally relies on foreign co-production to complete the funding. We are indebted to Tim Gardam, the director of programmes, for taking the decision that Channel Four should fully fund the production.

At Windfall Films special thanks are due to: Carlo Massarella who has contributed so much to the book and the television series; Ian Duncan and Jim Burge who directed the first three programmes; assistant producer, Gerald Lorenz; editors, Paul Shepard, Tim Cawston and Ian Meller; production manager Marisa Verazzo and Ruby Evans who looked after an enormously complex schedule and budget. Meticulous research was carried out by Leesa Rumley, Robert Hartell and Xavier Alford. We would also like to praise our fixers: Chako Sugi-Bellamy in Japan, Zhang Yong Ning in China and Anita and Tek Gurung in Nepal.

Finally, we must thank Alan Macfarlane and his wife Sarah Harrison who have been so generous with their time and hospitality. It has been a very special and enjoyable collaboration. Ever since the first meeting, Alan has been at the hub of this project. His breadth and depth of knowledge never ceased to amaze us. Always patient with our misconceptions and ignorance, he read early drafts of all the chapters and gently guided and encouraged us.

INDEX

PICTURE CREDITS

While every effort has been made to trace copyright holders for photographs and illustrations featured in the book, the publishers will be glad to make proper acknowledgements in future editions in the event that any regrettable omissions have occurred at the time of going to press.

2: Mann Collection. 4 (left), 6–7, 7 (right), 106–07, 118, 122, 123, 128, 133, 137, 156, 159, 168: David Dugan. 4 (middle), 68: National Trust Photographic Library/Wallington. 4 (right), 73: *The Return to Amsterdam of the Fleet of the Dutch East India Company in 1599* (oil on copper) by Andries van Eertvelt (1590–1652) Johnny can Haeften Gallery, London, UK/Bridgeman Art Library. 5 (left), 105: © Adam Woolfitt/CORBIS. 5 (middle), 149: *The Great Wall of China*, from *China in a Series of Views* by George Newenham Wright (c.1790–1877) 1843 (coloured engraving) by Thomas Allom (1804–72) (after) Private Collection/The Stapleton Collection/Bridgeman Art Library. 5 (right), 66, 158: The Art Archive. 9: Channel 4. 10, 13, 24, 27, 28, 30, 31, 32, 33: National Railway Museum/Science & Society. 11: Mander & Mitchenson Theatre Collection. 15: *Liverpool Docks* by John Atkinson Grimshaw (1836–93) Whitford & Hughes, London, UK/Bridgeman Art Library. 17, 36, 40, 50, 100, 127: Mary Evans Picture Library. 19, 34: Mansell/Time Inc./Katz. 21: Helmshore Textile Museums & Blackburn Borough Council. 22–23: Marisa Verazzo. 25, 53: Hulton Getty. 26, 43, 48, 91, 180–181: Science Museum/Science & Society Picture Library. 37: *A View of the Whitechapel Road*, from the *Progress of Steam*, 1828 by Henry Thomas Alken (1785–1851) National Railway Museum, York, North Yorkshire, UK/Bridgeman Art Library. 38–39: © Paul Almasy/CORBIS. 45, 46: Ironbridge Gorge Museum Trust. 55, 56, 57, 58–59, 60, 62, 62–63: Trustees of The Wedgwood Museum, Barlaston, Staffordshire (England). 67: *Loyal Addresses and Radical Petitions*, 1819 by George Cruikshank (1792–1878) Guildhall Library, Corporation of London, UK/Bridgeman Art Library. 69: *Dr Livingstone's Remains at Southampton: Procession to the Railway Station*, from *The Illustrated London News*, 25 April 1874 (engraving) (b/w photo) by English School (19th century) Private Collection/The Stapleton Collection/Bridgeman Art Library. 70–71: *The Shore at Egmond-aan-Zee* by Jacob van Ruisdael © National Gallery, London. 72: Tate Gallery/The Art Archive. 75: *Flowers in a vase* (panel) by Johannes Antonius van der Baren (c.1615–86) Johannesburg Art Gallery, South Africa/Bridgeman Art Library. 76 (left): *Four Officers of the Amsterdam Coopers' and Wine-rackers' Guild* by Gerbrand van den Eeckhout © National Gallery, London. 76–77: *A Windmill by a River* by Jan van Goyen © National Gallery. 78–79: The Fotomas Index UK. 81: *Samuel Pepys (1633–1703)* (engraving) (b&w photo) by Sir Godfrey Kneller (1646–1723) (after) Private Collection/Bridgeman Art Library. 83: *The Royal Exchange and the Bank of England*, lithograph by T. Picken, printed by Day & Son, published by Rudolph Ackerman, 1851 (colour litho) by George Sidney Shepherd (1784–1862) (after) Guildhall Library, Corporation of London, UK/Bridgeman Art Library. 85: © Ally Meyer/CORBIS. 87: *Battle of Vienna, 1683, 14 July – 12 Sept.: Turks besiege Vienna, 12 Sept., Charles of Lorraine defeats the Turks at the Kahlenberg, near Vienna*, British Library, London, UK/Bridgeman Art Library. 89: Col. NMM, photo © Michael Holford. 90: © National Maritime Museum, London. 94: *Map of Australia/Carte des Australes*: The British Library (Neg. 1051 Or 503, Shelfmk. K.Top.IV., Pg/Fol: 60). 95: *Sir Joseph Banks, 1773, Botanist* by Benjamin West (1738–1820) Lincolnshire County Council, Usher Gallery, Lincoln, UK/Bridgeman Art Gallery. 96: *Transplanting of the bread fruit trees from Otaheite (Tahiti)*, engraved and published by the artist, 1796 (mezzotint) by Thomas Gosse (1765–1844) National Library of Australia, Canberra, Australia/Bridgeman Art Library. 99, 170–71: Mike Coles. 102: Cambridge University Press. 109: Domestic clock with foliot escapement, probably made in Germany, 15th century. The Worshipful Company of Clockmakers' Collection, UK/Bridgeman Art Library. 110: From *De Re Metallica* (Dover Publications, 1950). 116 (left) *Self Portrait at the Age of 34* by Rembrandt © National Gallery, London. 116 (right): *Self Portrait at the Age of 63* by Rembrandt © National Gallery, London. 119: © Royal Ontario Museum/CORBIS. 120: *Portrait of Matteo Ricci (1552–1610)* Italian missionary, founder of the Jesuit mission in China (panel) by Italian School (17th century) Gesu, Rome, Italy/Bridgeman Art Library. 121: *Forbidden City, Peking*, 1980 (aquatint and etching) by Patrick Procktor (b.1936) Redfern Gallery, London, UK/Bridgeman Art Library. 124–25: *The Transept of the Crystal Palace from the Grand Entrance, 1851* (chromolitho) by W.H. Simpson (fl.1880) (after) Guildhall Library, Corporation of London, UK/Bridgeman Art Library. 129: MSI. 131, 132, 146, 165: Christopher Dugan. 134–35: *Ploughing* (pencil and pastel on ivorine) by Cecil Charles Windsor Aldin (1870–1935) Private Collection/The British Sporting Art Trust/Bridgeman Art Library, © Anthony C. Mason. 139: Musée des Arts Asiatiques – Guimet, Paris © Photo RMN – Michel Urtado. 142, 143: The Board of Trustees of the National Museums & Galleries on Merseyside. 145: *The Invention of Gunpowder and the First Casting of Bronze Cannon*, plate 4 from *Nova Reperta* (New Discoveries) engraved by Philip Galle (1537–1612) c.1600 (engraving) by Jan van der Straet (Giovanni Stradano) (1523–1605) (after) Private Collection/The Stapleton Collection/Bridgeman Art Library. 147: *Venice: The Basin of San Marco on Ascension Day* by Canaletto © National Gallery, London. 150, 161: © Copyright The British Museum. 151: © Betmann/CORBIS. 152: © CORBIS. 154: Photo: Fukuzawa Memorial Center for Modern Japanese Studies, Keio University. 163: ML Design. 169: *Sheep and Goat* by Chao Meng-Fu (1254–1322), (ink on paper mounted on silk) Yuan Dynasty, (1260–1368) Freer Gallery, Smithsonian Institution, Washington, USA/Bridgeman Art Library. 171: From *Chinese Technology in the Seventeenth Century* (Dover Publications, 1966). 173: *Three Prize Pigs outside a Sty* by English School (19th century) Iona Antiques, London, UK/Bridgeman Art Library. 174: © Charles & Josette Lenars/CORBIS. 176: National Museum of American Art, Washington DC/Art Resource, NY. 177: *Across the Continent: 'Westward the Course of Empire Takes its Way'*, pub. by Currier and Ives, New York, 1868 (litho) by F.E. Palmer (19th century) (after) Museum of the City of New York, USA/Bridgeman Art Library. 178: *Herd of Bison, near Lake Jessie* by John Mix Stanley, 1860, toned lithograph, no. 1964.58 Amon Carter Museum, Fort Worth, Texas. 179 (neg. no. ICHi–05656), 180 (neg. no. ICHi–29619), 183 (neg. no. ICHi–01622) Courtesy of Chicago Historical Society. 182: From the collections of Henry Ford Museum & Greenfield Village. 184: © Jeremy Horner/CORBIS. 184–85: © Kevin R. Morris/CORBIS. 186–187, 187: UFA (Courtesy Kobal).